MORE TADPOLE TALES AND OTHER TOTALLY TERRIFIC TREATS FOR READERS THEATRE

RECENT TITLES IN TEACHER IDEAS PRESS' READERS THEATRE SERIES

MORE TADPOLE TALES AND OTHER TOTALLY TERRIFIC TREATS FOR READERS THEATRE

Anthony D. Fredericks

Readers Theatre

A Teacher Ideas Press Book

LIBRARIES UNLIMITED

AN IMPRINT OF ABC-CLIO, LLC
Santa Barbara, California • Denver, Colorado • Oxford, England

Library of Congress Cataloging-in-Publication Data

Fredericks, Anthony D.
  More tadpole tales and other totally terrific treats for readers theatre / Anthony D. Fredericks.
     p. cm.
  Includes bibliographical references and index.
   ISBN 978-1-59884-382-8 (pbk : alk. paper) — ISBN 978-1-59884-383-5 (ebook) 1. Readers'
theater. 2. Mother Goose—Parodies, imitations, etc. 3. Fairy tales—Parodies, imitations, etc. I. Title.
PN2081.R4F741 2010
398.2—dc22   2010028160

ISBN: 978-1-59884-382-8

E-ISBN: 978-1-59884-383-5

14 13 12 11 10   1 2 3 4 5

This book is also available on the World Wide Web as an eBook.
Visit www.abc-clio.com for details.

Libraries Unlimited
An Imprint of ABC-CLIO, LLC

ABC-CLIO, LLC
130 Cremona Drive, P.O. Box 1911
Santa Barbara, California 93116-1911

This book is printed on acid-free paper ∞
Manufactured in the United States of America

Contents

Some Authors Add This Little Section (Which They Call a Preface) to a Book to Tell You Some Things About How (or Why) the Book Was Written . . . So, I Guess I Will Too!

You see, once upon a time, way back in 1997 I wrote a book called *Tadpole Tales and Other Totally Terrific Treats for Readers Theatre*. That book came on the heels of another book I wrote for Teacher Ideas Press, *Frantic Frogs and Other Frankly Fractured Folktales for Readers Theatre*—a book that was hugely successful then and is still selling a ton of copies . . . even today.

Tadpole Tales and Other Totally Terrific Treats for Readers Theatre grew out of several conversations I had had with classroom teachers and librarians around the country who wanted some readers theatre materials for kids in the primary grades. And so I created a collection of scripts written at various readability levels that could be easily integrated into the language arts curriculum or the overall library program. Titles of some of the scripts in that book included:

❖ "Mary Had a Little Lamb That Made a Big 'No-No' on the Classroom Floor"

❖ "Little Miss Muffet sat on a Tuffet and Squashed a Poor Little Spider"

❖ "Old Mother Hubbard Went to the Cupboard and Got Sick at What She Saw"

❖ "Rub-a-Dub Dub, How Did All Those Guys Get in That Tub?"

❖ "Jack and Jill Don't Understand Why They have to Go Up and Down a Hill"

❖ "Here We Go Round the Mulberry Bush and I'm Sure Getting Dizzy"

(It should be clearly evident that my sense of humor is completely irreverent, incredibly warped, and totally off the wall—a fact any of my students will gladly verify.)

Anyway, after I wrote *Tadpole Tales,* . . . it soon found its way into catalogs, Web sites, bookstores, and lots of educational conferences around the country. It wasn't long before the book was selling like the proverbial stack of hotcakes. Teachers would buy it and use it as a major part of their language arts programs. Librarians would buy it and use it to introduce familiar fairy tales and legends as part of numerous library projects. Homeschoolers would buy it to spice up family discussions and instructional opportunities.

Every once in a while I would receive letters, e-mails, and personal comments from teachers, librarians, and kids who became fans of the book and who would mention the unbelievable joy and unmatched hilarity that was so much a part of those scripts. One teacher wrote, "My students gave up recess for two whole days just so they could do more scripts!" Another wrote, "I love teaching language arts now—my students are really into readers theatre!" A third grade teacher in Colorado recently told me that her students were inspired to write their own readers theatre script, entitled "American Tadpole" (a take-off on *American Idol*).

With the success of *Tadpole Tales and Other Totally Terrific Treats for Readers Theatre*, dozens of teachers and librarians would approach me during my author visits or teacher in-service programs to their schools asking for another volume of wild and wacky readers theatre scripts (of course, there were others who approached me asking for small loans—but that's another story altogether.). They asked for (and, in some cases, demanded) another volume of absurd, ridiculous, humorous, preposterous, comical, outlandish, amusing, hilarious, nonsensical, and totally insane readers theatre scripts they could use in their classrooms and libraries.

Thus was born the idea for this book—a collection of MORE crazy, irreverent, demented, outrageous, gross, and just-plain-funny scripts kids in grades 1–4 can use as part of their language arts programs. I hope you will discover—as have thousands of teachers and librarians all over the country—that readers theatre can be a wonderful way to show students "language in action." I think you will find that humor has a real and important place in the classroom and school library; and what better way to make that concept a natural and normal part of any elementary program than through the magic and energy of readers theatre?

I had a lot of fun writing the first *Tadpole Tales . . . .* book, and you should know that that convoluted view of traditional children's stories and fairy tale characters has been continued in the pages of this "*MORE*" volume. I sincerely hope that you find the scripts in this book to be as welcome and amusing as those in the first volume and that they will "energize" your students with an overwhelming abundance of hilarity, humor, amusement, fun, jocularity, and infectious good times.

Here's to lots of laughter, lots of learning, and lots of just plain craziness!!! May your classroom or library be filled with all three.

Tony Fredericks

Here's the Introduction Part of the Book That Gives You Some Pretty Important Stuff That You Gotta Know Before You Read the Other Stuff in the Book. (But Don't Worry; You Won't Have to Take a Test on This Stuff or Anything Like That!)

Say the words "Once upon a time. . . ." to any adult, and you will probably see a smile slip across his or her face. Those are magical words—words that conjure up stories of long ago. For most of us, they bring back pleasant memories of someone (our parents or a favorite teacher) reading (aloud) a story or book. Those words may remind us of simpler times—times long before we had to worry about home mortgages, saving for our kid's college tuition, retirement plans, or even behavioral objectives. The memories were sweet, and the recollections were always pleasurable.

Think how those same four words might affect the students with whom you work. Think of the mental journeys or creative adventures you can share with youngsters as you lead them through the magical world of children's literature. Imaginations are stimulated and minds are filled with the delicious sounds of language in action! It is that language—the language of feeling, emotion, and passion—that excites youngsters and helps them appreciate the role literature and books play in their everyday lives (as they have for generations).

And what better way to bring children's literature alive than through the magic of readers theatre? Readers theatre offers youngsters interesting and unique insights into the utility of language and its value in both its printed and oral forms. It is "language arts" in its purest form: It boosts listening and speaking skills, enhances writing abilities, powers reading development, develops positive self-concepts, and transforms reluctant readers into energized readers. Quite simply, it is literature brought to life and life brought to literature.

WHAT YOUR PRINCIPAL NEEDS TO KNOW

In this era of accountability and standards-based education, many educators want to know if classroom practices—whether traditional or innovative—have an impact on the literacy growth of students. Significant research on the use of readers theatre in elementary classrooms has demonstrated its positive effects on comprehension development, motivation to read, attitudes toward learning, and appreciation of reading as a lifelong skill.

What follows is a brief summary of some significant research on the impact of readers theatre on the literacy growth of students. Please feel free to share this information with interested administrators, parents, or community members. Suffice it to say, readers theatre is a "research-based practice" that has been demonstrated to have a significant and powerful impact on students' reading growth and development.

❖ "Creative and critical thinking are enhanced through the utilization of readers theatre. Children are active participants in the interpretation and delivery of a story; as such, they develop thinking skills that are divergent rather than convergent, and interpretive skills that are supported rather than directed." (Fredericks 2007)

❖ "Readers theatre provides an active, analytical framework for reading and helps students to understand and interpret what they read." (Wolf 1998)

❖ "Readers theatre provides troubled readers with successful reading experiences; it can reshape images of failure into those of success and accomplishment. Readers theatre forms a bridge between troubled reading to supported reading, and ultimately, independent reading." (Dixon et al. 1996)

❖ "Readers theatre [promotes] oral reading fluency, as children [explore] and [interpret] the meaning of literature." (Martinez et al. 1999)

❖ "We are gaining evidence from classroom research that readers theatre yields improvements in students' word recognition, fluency, and comprehension." (Rasinski 2003)

❖ "[Readers theatre] is valuable for non-English speaking children or non-fluent readers. Readers theatre provides them with positive models of language usage and interpretation. . . . It allows them to see 'language in action' and the various ways in which language can be used." (Fredericks 2001)

❖ "Even resistant readers eagerly engage in practicing for readers theatre performance, reading and rereading scripts many times (Tyler and Chard 2000)

❖ "Second graders who did readers theatre on a regular basis made, on average, more than a year's growth in reading." (Strecker et al. 1999)

❖ "As students take on the roles of characters [in readers theatre], they also take on the roles of competent readers." (Fredericks 2008a, 2008b)

The research is clear: Classroom teachers and librarians who make readers theatre a regular and systematic component of their literacy instruction and introduction to literature will be providing those students with positive opportunities to succeed in all aspects of reading growth and development. Word recognition, vocabulary, fluency, and comprehension can all be enhanced considerably when readers theatre becomes part of the educational offerings in any classroom or library.

WHAT IS THE VALUE OF READERS THEATRE?

Above and beyond the substantive research supporting the use of readers theatre as a positive classroom and library activity, here's what I like so much about readers theatre: It allows children to breathe life and substance into literature, an interpretation that is neither right nor wrong, since it will be colored by kids' unique perspectives, experiences, and vision. The reader's interpretation of a piece of literature intrinsically more valuable than some predetermined "translation" that might be found in a teacher's manual, for example.

Many teachers subscribe to the notion that reading involves an active and energetic relationship between the reader and the text. That is, the reader–text relationship is reciprocal and involves the characteristics of the reader as well as the nature of the material (Fredericks 2001). This philosophy of reading has particular applications for teachers and librarians building effective literacy programs. As you might expect, it also serves as a foundation for the implementation and effectiveness of readers theatre.

With that in mind, here are some of the many educational values I see in readers theatre. These have come from my own work with youngsters as a former classroom teacher and reading specialist, a thorough review of the literature on readers theatre, as well as my observations of, and conversations with, classroom teachers throughout the United States and Canada.

1. Readers theatre brings literature to life! For many students, particularly those struggling with reading, words on a page often appear as "lifeless characters"—devoid of expression, emotion, or involvement. Readers theatre, however, provides both accomplished and struggling readers with a lively and active interpretation of books. Readers get to see and participate in a personal interpretation and involvement process that "activates" the words, characters, and plots of stories.

2. Students are connected to real literature in authentic situations. They are exposed to quality literature from a wide range of authors and a wide range of genres. Many readers theatre scripts are based on real literature sources, and students can begin developing their own interpretations of literature through the creation of their own scripts based on those books. In fact, one of the best ways to help children enjoy and extend their appreciation of good books is by encouraging them to write and perform readers theatre productions after reading an appropriate piece of literature. Readers theatre can also be used to introduce children to good literature. After performing a readers theatre script, children will be stimulated to read the original source, not to compare, but rather to extend their learning opportunities. In short, readers theatre may precede the reading of a related book or be used as an appropriate follow-up to the reading (oral or silent) of a good book. Quality literature and readers theatre are mutually complementary elements of the overall literacy program that underscore children's active engagement in text.

3. Children can learn about the major features of children's literature: plot, theme, setting, point of view, and characterization. This occurs when they are provided with opportunities to design and construct their own readers theatre scripts (after experiencing prepared scripts such as those in this book or scripts that you create using books and literature shared in regular reading instruction).

4. Readers theatre helps students focus on the integration of all of the language arts: reading, writing, speaking, and listening. Children begin to see that effective communication and the comprehension of text are inexorably intertwined. Most state standards in the language arts, and all research reports about best practices in literacy, underscore literacy as an integrated series of related components. In other words, literacy growth is not just growth in reading—it is

the development of reading in concert with the other language arts. The section below ("Hey, What about Standards") provides the specific connections between each of the English/language arts standards and readers theatre. It's interesting to note how readers theatre promotes, enhances, and solidifies students' mastery of all 12 *Standards for the English Language Arts*.

5. Teachers and librarians have also discovered that readers theatre is an excellent way to enhance the development of important communication skills. Voice projection, intonation, inflection, and pronunciation skills are all promoted throughout any readers theatre production. This places more value on the processes of literacy instruction than on the products (e.g., standardized test scores).

6. Readers theatre allows children to experience stories in a supportive and nonthreatening format that underscores their active involvement. This is particularly beneficial for those students who are struggling with reading. Struggling readers often envision reading as something "done *to* a text" rather than as something "done *with* a text." This shift in perspective is often a critical factor in the success youngsters can eventually enjoy in reading. A change in attitude, a change in viewpoint, and a change in purpose often lead below-level readers to some new and interesting discoveries. Motivation, confidence, and outlook are all positively affected when students become the players and the performers. Equally important, the development and enhancement of self-concept is facilitated through readers theatre. Because children are working in concert with other children in a supportive atmosphere, their self-esteem mushrooms accordingly.

7. Readers theatre stimulates the imagination and the creation of visual images. A process of mental imagery helps readers construct "mind pictures" that serve as a way to tie together predictions, background knowledge, and textual knowledge in a satisfying experience. Once images are created, they become a permanent part of long-term memory. Just as important, they assist in the development of independent readers who are "connected" with the stories they read. It has been substantiated that when youngsters are provided with opportunities to create their own mental images, their comprehension and appreciation of a piece of writing will be enhanced considerably.

8. The central goal of reading instruction is comprehension. Comprehension is based on one's ability to make sense of printed materials. It goes beyond one's ability to remember details or recall factual information from text. Several researchers (Wiggens and McTighe 1998; Wiske 1998) suggest that students comprehend when they are able to a) connect new knowledge to their prior knowledge, b) interpret what they learn, c) apply their knowledge to new situations, and d) explain and predict events and actions. Readers theatre provides students with rich opportunities to accomplish all four elements of reading comprehension in a learning environment that is both supportive and engaged. Giving meaning to print is one of the major results of readers theatre, just as it is one of the major results of comprehension instruction.

9. Cunningham and Allington (2003) have shown that readers theatre is a perfect multilevel activity that allows teachers to group students heterogeneously rather than by ability, as is done in traditional reading programs. It provides teachers with varied options to group students by interest and desire rather than by reading level. Parts can be assigned that are sufficiently challenging (instructional level) without forcing students to deal with material at their frustration level of reading. Since students will have multiple opportunities to practice their "reading materials" at an appropriate level, they will be able to achieve levels of both competence and fluency not normally provided in more traditional, "round robin" reading activities.

10. Readers theatre is a participatory event. The characters as well as the audience are all intimately involved in the design, structure, and delivery of the story. Children begin to realize that reading is not a solitary activity, but rather one that can be shared and discussed with others. As a result, readers theatre enhances the development of cooperative learning strategies.

Not only does readers theatre require youngsters to work together toward a common goal, but even more important, it supports their efforts in doing so.

11. Because it is the performance that drives readers theatre, children are given more opportunities to invest themselves and their personalities in the production of a readers theatre. The same story may be subject to several different presentations depending on the group or the individual youngsters involved.

12. When children are provided with opportunities to write and/or script their own readers theatre, their writing abilities are supported and encouraged. As children become familiar with the design and format of readers theatre scripts, they can begin to utilize their own creative talents in designing their own scripts. Readers theatre also exposes students to many examples of quality literature. That literature serves as positive models for their own writing. Just as authors of children's books write for authentic purposes (e.g., to entertain, to inform, to convince), so too will students understand the value of purposeful writing as they craft original readers theatre scripts or adaptations from popular books and stories.

13. Readers theatre is fun! Children of all ages have delighted in using readers theatre for many years. It is delightful and stimulating, encouraging and fascinating, relevant and personal. It is a classroom or library activity filled with a cornucopia of instructional possibilities and educational ventures.

"HEY, WHAT ABOUT STANDARDS?"

In response to a demand for a cohesive set of standards that address overall curriculum design and comprehensive student performance expectations in reading and language arts education, the International Reading Association, in concert with the National Council of Teachers of English, developed and promulgated the IRA/NCTE *Standards for the English Language Arts*. These standards provide a focused outline of the essential components of a well-structured language arts curriculum.

The 12 standards place an emphasis on literacy development as a lifelong process—one that starts well before youngsters enter school and continues throughout their lives. Thus, these standards are intentionally integrative and multidisciplinary. Just as important, they support and underscore the value of readers theatre (see above) as a multipurpose language arts activity—one appropriate for both classroom and library.

The chart below provides an abridged version of the *Standards for the English Language Arts*. Along with each standard (as appropriate) is how readers theatre serves as a valuable and innovative teaching tool in support of that standards.

English/Language Arts Standards*	Readers Theatre Support
1. Students are engaged in a wide variety of print and nonprint resources.	Readers theatre introduces students to a wealth of literature from a variety of literary sources.
2. Students are exposed to many genres of literature.	Readers theatre offers students a range of reading materials that span the eight basic genres of children's literature.
3. Students use many reading strategies to comprehend text.	Readers theatre invites students to assume an active role in comprehension development through their engagement and participation.

English/Language Arts Standards*	Readers Theatre Support
4. Students communicate in a variety of ways.	Readers theatre invites students to practice reading, writing, listening, and speaking in an enjoyable and educative process.
5. Students learn through writing.	Readers theatre encourages students to develop their own scripts and share them with a receptive audience.
6. Students use a variety of language conventions to understand text.	Readers theatre encourages students to discuss and understand how language conveys ideas.
7. Students are involved in personally meaningful research projects.	Readers theatre invites youngsters to examine and explore stories from a wide range of perspectives.
8. Students are comfortable with technology.	Readers theatre provides opportunities for students to use technology to create, share, and disseminate classroom scripts.
9. Students gain an appreciation of language in a variety of venues.	Readers theatre encourages students to look at language and language use in a host of educational formats.
10. Non-English-speaking students develop competencies in all the language arts.	Readers theatre offers models of English use in a fun and engaging format.
11. Students are members of a host of literacy communities.	Readers theatre provides creative, investigative, and dynamic opportunities to see language in action.
12. Students use language for personal reasons.	Readers theatre offers innumerable opportunities for students to engage in personally enriching language activities.

*Modified and abridged from *Standards for the English Language Arts*, International Reading Association/National Council of Teachers of English, 1996

When reviewing these standards, it should become evident that many can be promoted through the regular and systematic introduction of readers theatre into the elementary language arts curriculum. Equally important, these standards assist teachers and librarians in validating the impact and significance of readers theatre as a viable and valuable instructional tool—in language arts and throughout the entire elementary curriculum.

PART I

This Is the Part That Shows up Near the Beginning of the Book (Which Is Why It's Called "Part I") and That Will Help You Be the Coolest Teacher or Librarian in Your School or District (or Maybe Even Your Entire State)

CHAPTER 1

Getting Started with Readers Theatre

INTRODUCING READERS THEATRE TO STUDENTS

Ever since I wrote my first book of readers theatre scripts—*Frantic Frogs and Other Frankly Fractured Folktales for Readers Theatre* (1993)—I have been amazed and delighted with the incredible response readers theatre has generated among educators across the country. Teachers in urban, suburban, and rural schools have all told me of the incredible power of readers theatre as a regular feature of their language arts or reading curricula. In more than one dozen subsequent teacher resource books on readers theatre (please see appendix E in the back of this book), I have shared (and seen) the passion and excitement that is so much a part of an elementary curriculum infused with readers theatre.

In the teacher in-service programs I conduct and conference workshops I present on readers theatre, I continue to receive rave reviews of readers theatre as a way of helping students take an active role in the reading process. Many teachers have commented about the improved levels of motivation and heightened participation in all aspects of the reading curriculum when readers theatre has been added to students' daily literacy activities.

However, readers theatre is not something that you just "drop into" the curriculum one day and expect students to enthusiastically embrace it. It must be introduced to students on a gradual basis—over the course of several days or several weeks—to achieve maximum impact. Of course, no two teachers will introduce readers theatre in exactly the same way. What follows is an instructional plan of action that allows for a great deal of latitude and variation depending on how your reading or language arts program is organized as well as the specific time constraints of your classroom or library schedule. Feel free to make any necessary adjustments or modifications in the schedule below to suit your personal philosophy or the specific instructional needs of your students.

My experience, as well as that of many teachers, is that students need to transition through four stages in order for readers theatre to become a viable component of the overall literacy program. These four stages follow:

1. **Introduction.** This is the stage at which students are first introduced to readers theatre. In cases where most students have been using readers theatre in previous grades, this stage can be eliminated.

2. **Familiarization.** In this stage students become comfortable with the concept of readers theatre. They begin to understand its value as an instructional tool as well as its worth in helping them become accomplished and fluent readers.

3. **Practice.** Here students are offered a variety of ways in which to practice readers theatre in authentic situations. Students begin to see positive growth and development in both reading fluency and comprehension.

4. **Integration.** This stage provides students with regular and systematic opportunities to use readers theatre as a significant element in other aspects of the reading or library program (e.g., guided reading, literature circles) as well as other subject areas (e.g., science, social studies).

What follows are some suggested instructional activities and presentations to share with your students. These suggestions are general in nature and can be easily incorporated into one or more lesson plans. Again, depending on the dynamics of your overall classroom reading program or library program, the lessons may last for as little as 10 minutes or as much as one hour.

1. **Introduction** (suggested duration: 1–3 days)

    A.   Select a prepared readers theatre script. Choose one of the scripts from this book or from any other readers theatre collection of scripts (see appendix C). Duplicate sufficient copies of the script for every member of the class.

    B.   Distribute the scripts to students. Tell students that a readers theatre script is exactly like a script used by actors in television, the movies, or plays. The only difference is that in readers theatre the lines don't have to be memorized. Nevertheless, they still have to be read with the same level of enthusiasm and emotion that professional actors use.

    C.   Identify and discuss the various printed elements of the script. Identify the narrator, the staging instructions, how the various actor parts are designated, any emotional suggestions noted for specific characters, and other features.

    D.   Invite students to silently read through the script on their own. You may wish to use the script as part of a guided reading lesson. Afterward, ask student to share what they noted in the script (e.g., a narrator, a different style of writing, short parts and long parts). Record students' observations on the chalkboard and plan time to discuss them.

E. Use the script as a read-aloud for your students. Tell students that you are going to model how a readers theatre script should be read. Inform them that you will also be modeling fluent and expressive reading. You will add emotion to certain parts and will maintain a consistent rate throughout the reading, as well. Invite students to listen carefully to this initial reading.

F. After reading through the script, invite students to discuss what they heard. How did your reading differ from other read-alouds in the classroom? How was it similar? What did they enjoy about your reading? How might they have presented the script? Record their observations on the chalkboard.

G. As appropriate, show students another prepared readers theatre script. Invite them to identify selected elements of the script (narrator, specific characters, staging directions, etc.). Make sure students understand that most readers theatre scripts follow a fairly standard format.

2. Familiarization (suggested duration: 1 week)

Before engaging students in this stage, you may wish to select 5 to 10 lines or passages from a forthcoming script. It is suggested that these lines or passages come from the beginning of the script and that they be representative of most (if not all) of the characters (including any narrator[s]). Record these passages on cardboard sentence strips (using block printing or a word processing program).

Here are some sample sentence strips from the beginning of the readers theatre script "The Old Woman and All Those Kids":

NARRATOR	Once upon a time there was an old woman who lived in a shoe.
OLD WOMAN	Hey, how come I have to live in a shoe?
NARRATOR	I don't know, lady. I'm just here to tell the story.
OLD WOMAN	Yeah, but I don't want to live in a shoe.
NARRATOR	Sorry, I can't help you. I'm just reading what the author put here in the script.

After creating the necessary sentence strips, engage students in the following sequence of activities:

A. Select a prepared readers theatre script (one from this book, for example, or any other collection of scripts). Record the script on audiotape (you may wish to alter your voice slightly for each of the characters or you may wish to enlist the aid of some other teachers, or parents, to help you record the script). Make sure this recording of the script is fluent and smooth (practice several times if necessary).

B. Provide students with copies of the selected script. Point out, once more, how a readers theatre script is organized (e.g., narrator, individual characters, etc.). Tell students that they will listen to a reading of the script on an audiotape.

C. Play the recording for students. Invite them to listen carefully for the smooth and fluent reading. Encourage them, as appropriate, to follow along by pointing to each word as they hear it.

D. You may wish to repeat the sequence above, particularly if you are using this sequence with a group of struggling readers who may need some additional reinforcement and assistance.

E. Provide an opportunity for students to discuss what they heard, the intonation exhibited by the readers, the smoothness of their delivery, or any other aspects of the recording. You may wish to record these observations on the chalkboard or a sheet of newsprint.

F. Invite the class (or group) to read through the entire script chorally. You should also participate in this choral reading so that students have a positive model and an appropriate support system for their oral reading. At this stage, it would be appropriate to emphasize the emotions that selected characters may bring to their parts (e.g., anger, disgust, happiness).

G. After the choral reading, randomly distribute the sentence strips to selected students. Inform the students that they will now become the characters in the play. Invite the students to stand in a line. Point to each character (using the sequence in the script) and invite each student to read his or her selected passage.

H. Invite other students to listen and comment (in a positive way) about the presentation of the first part of the script.

I. Distribute the sentence strips to another group of students and invite them to line up and recite the passages as the previous group did. Again, it would be appropriate to discuss the nature of the presentation in a supportive atmosphere.

J. (optional) Play the recorded version of the script again for the students. Invite them to make any additional comments.

3. Practice (suggested duration: 1–2 weeks)

A. Select, duplicate, and distribute a prepared script to all the students in your class. *Note:* At this particular stage I have frequently given students a selection of two to three possible scripts from which the entire class makes a single choice. This gives students a sense of ownership over the script, which ultimately results in a heightened level of motivation.

B. Divide the class into pairs or triads of students. Invite students to share the script in their small groups. Students may wish to read the script silently after, which they may discuss the story line, characters, plot, or other elements. Students may also elect to read certain sections to each other, not only to practice fluent reading, but also to get a "feel" for the story.

C. Assign roles. I like to assign one student from each of the small groups to a character in the script. (If there are, for example, six characters, I make sure that students are initially divided into six small groups). Each character then practices his or her part with the other members of his or her group (for example, the character reads only his or her lines to group members who assist with any difficult words or comment on the fluency of the reading).

D. When students have had sufficient practice, arrange them according to the staging directions for that script.

E. Invite the assigned students to read through the script just as they practiced it. Invite others students to listen to the presentation. After the script is completed, discuss how it might be improved the next time.

F.   (optional) Reassign roles to different students in the class. Divide the class into small groups and repeat the sequence as described above.

4.   **Integration** (suggested duration: remainder of the school year or remainder of the unit)

A.   Select a prepared readers theatre script (one from this book or any other collection of scripts listed in appendix A). Assign roles to selected students and distribute copies of the scripts to those students. You may wish to use two or three separate scripts—each distributed to a different group of students in the class.

B.   Invite students to practice their assigned parts in preparation for a production later on. Students should be provided with practice time in class and should also be encouraged to practice their respective parts at home.

C.   Schedule a day and time when students will present their scripts to others in the class. This initial presentation should be kept as an in-class presentation to allay any fears students may have about presenting to an unfamiliar group of individuals. Ask students if they would like to invite their parents to attend this presentation.

D.   After presenting the initial script, invite students to select other prepared scripts for a more formal presentation.

E.   Invite students to create their own readers theatre scripts from self-selected literature in the classroom or school library. Make this process a normal part of your writing program or a basic element of a writer's workshop. After students have created their own scripts, provide them with opportunities to present them to appropriate audiences, including classrooms at a grade level above or below yours.

F.   Consider the implementation of readers theatre a fundamental element in literature circles. After students have engaged in a discussion about a self-selected book, invite them to develop the book into a readers theatre script that can become a permanent part of the classroom library.

G.   Students may wish to use readers theatre as part of a thematic unit. According to Meinbach et al., "a thematic approach to learning combines structured, sequential, and well-organized strategies, activities, children's literature, and materials used to expand a particular concept" (2000, 10). Readers theatre has the advantage of offering youngsters a creative and dynamic way to utilize their reading abilities in a productive and engaging manner. By integrating readers theatre into thematic units, you will help students gain a deeper appreciation of the role of reading (and reading fluency) in their overall literacy development.

H.   Use prepared scripts or student-created scripts as part of your content area instruction. Readers theatre has been shown to stimulate curiosity (when used in advance of a content area unit) and promote enthusiasm (when used as part of an instructional unit), particularly when incorporated into a variety of subject areas (Fredericks 2007).

I.   Readers theatre can be effectively incorporated into guided reading activities in any classroom. The three critical and interrelated stages of guided reading (before reading, during reading, and after reading) offer you and your students unique opportunities to weave readers theatre into the overall reading curriculum. Imagine the thrill and excitement of students using a self-designed script as the reading selection in a guided reading group! Readers theatre holds the promise of helping students in a guided reading group understand and appreciate the richness of language, the ways in which to interpret that language, and how language can be a powerful vehicle for the comprehension and appreciation of different forms of literature (Fredericks 2001).

CHAPTER 2

Performing Readers Theatre for an Audience

One of the features of readers theatre I enjoy very much is the many ways in which it can become part of the classroom curriculum. Along with scores of other teachers, I've discovered that readers theatre can be a wonderful opportunity for students to become active participants in the entire learning process as well as engaged explorers of every curricular area.

Obviously, readers theatre achieves its greatest potency when students have multiple opportunities to share it with others. This chapter focuses on ways you can make that experience incredibly successful.

SCRIPT PREPARATION

One of the advantages of using readers theatre in the classroom or library is the lack of extra work or preparation time necessary to get "up and running." By using the scripts in this book, your preparation time is minimal.

❖ After a script has been selected for presentation make sufficient copies. A copy of the script should be provided for each actor. In addition, making two or three extra copies (one for you and "replacement" copies for scripts that are accidentally damaged or lost) is also a good idea. Copies for the audience are unnecessary and are not suggested.

❖ Bind each script between two sheets of colored construction paper or poster board. Bound scripts tend to formalize the presentation a little and lend an air of professionalism to the actors.

❖ Highlight each character's speaking parts with different color highlighter pens. This helps youngsters track their parts without being distracted by the dialogue of others.

STAGING

Staging involves the physical location of the readers as well as any necessary movements. Unlike in a more formal play, the movements are often minimal. The emphasis is more on presentation and less on action.

❖ For most presentations, readers will stand or sit on stools or chairs. The physical location of each reader has been indicated for each of the scripts in this book.

❖ If there are many characters in the presentation, it may be advantageous to have characters in the rear (upstage) standing while those in the front (downstage) are placed on stools or chairs. This ensures that the audience will both see and hear every actor.

❖ Usually all of the characters will be on stage throughout the duration of the presentation. For most presentations it is not necessary to have characters enter and exit. If you place the characters on stools, they may face the audience when they are involved in a particular scene and then turn around whenever they are not involved in a scene.

❖ Make simple, hand-lettered signs with the name of each character. Loop a piece of string or yarn through each sign and hang it around the neck of each respective character. That way, the audience will know the identity of each character throughout the presentation.

❖ Each reader will have her or his own copy of the script in a cover (see above). If possible, use a music stand for each reader's script (this allows readers to use their hands for dramatic interpretations as necessary).

❖ Several presentations have a narrator to set up the story. The narrator serves to establish the place and time of the story for the audience so that the characters can "jump into" their parts from the beginning of the story. Typically, the narrator is separated from the other "actors" and can be identified by a simple sign.

PROPS

Two of the positive features of readers theatre are its ease of preparation and its ease of presentation. Informality is a hallmark of any readers theatre script.

❖ Much of the setting for a story should take place in the audience's mind. Elaborate scenery is not necessary; simple props are often the best. For example:

   – A branch or potted plant may serve as a tree.
   – A drawing on the chalkboard may illustrate a building.
   – A hand-lettered sign may designate one part of the staging area as a particular scene (e.g., swamp, castle, field, forest).
   – Children's toys may be used for uncomplicated props (e.g., telephone, vehicles, etc.).
   – A sheet of aluminum foil or a remnant of blue cloth may be used to simulate a lake or pond.

❖ Costumes for the actors are unnecessary. A few simple items may be suggested by students. For example:

  – Hats, scarves, or aprons may be used by major characters.

  – A paper cutout may serve as a tie, button, or badge.

  – Old clothing (borrowed from parents) may be used as warranted.

❖ Some teachers and librarians have discovered that the addition of appropriate background music or sound effects enhances a readers theatre presentation.

❖ It's important to remember that the emphasis in readers theatre is on the reading, not on any accompanying "features." The best presentations are often the simplest.

DELIVERY

I've often found it advantageous to let students know that the only difference between a readers theatre presentation and a movie role is that they will have a script in their hands. This allows them to focus more on presenting a script rather than memorizing a script.

❖ When first introduced to readers theatre, students often have a tendency to "read into" their scripts. Encourage students to look up from their scripts and interact with other characters or the audience as appropriate.

❖ Practicing the script beforehand can eliminate the problem of students burying their heads in the pages. Children will understand the need to involve the audience as much as possible in the development of the story.

❖ Voice projection and delivery are important in allowing the audience to understand character actions. The proper mood and intent need to be established, which is possible when children are familiar and comfortable with each character's "style."

❖ Again, the emphasis is on delivery, so be sure to suggest different types of voice (i.e., angry, irritated, calm, frustrated, excited, etc.) that children may wish to use for their particular character(s).

SCRIPT SELECTION

Although several presentation options are listed in the box on p. 12, one of the best is when several different groups of students in your classroom come together to present a selection of readers theatre scripts for an audience of enthusiastic students (from the same or a different grade) and some very appreciative parents. Here are some possibilities for you to consider:

❖ When possible, invite students to select a variety of scripts to be included in the presentation. Inform them that a combination of short scripts and longer scripts adds variety to the program. When students are invited to be part of the selection process a sense of "ownership" develops, which contributes to the ultimate success of the overall presentation(s).

❖ Consider the age and grade of the audience. For younger students (grades K–2) the total program should be no longer than 20 minutes (a mix of two to four scripts). For older students (grades 3–6) the total program should be no longer than 45 minutes (a mix of four to five scripts).

❖ If feasible, include a section of the program (parts of a script or an entire production) in which the audience takes an active role. This could include singing, clapping, repeating selected lines in a production (provide cue cards), or some other physical contribution. This would be particularly appropriate for younger audiences, whose attention span is typically short and sporadic.

"IT'S SHOW TIME!"

After scripts have been selected by you and your students, it's time to consider how, when, and where you would like to present them. There are many options to consider. The following list, which is not all-inclusive, presents a variety of presentation options for readers theatre. How you and your students present readers theatre will ultimately be determined by the nature of your overall language arts program, the time and facilities available, the comfort level of students, and the demands of your overall curriculum. You will certainly discover that there is an almost inexhaustible array of options available.

Suggested Presentation Options for Readers Theatre

❖ One group of students presents a script to another group.

❖ One group of students presents to the entire class.

❖ Several groups of students present to the entire class (an in-class "readers theatre festival").

❖ One group of students presents to another class at the same grade level.

❖ Several groups of students present to another class at the same grade level.

❖ One group of students presents to a class at a higher or lower grade level.

❖ Several groups of students present to a class at a higher or lower grade level.

❖ One group of students presents to the entire school (at an all-school assembly).

❖ Several groups of students present to the entire school (at an all-school assembly).

❖ One group of students in the class presents to an audience of parents, school personnel, the school principal, and other interested individuals.

❖ Several groups of students in the class present to an audience of parents, school personnel, the school principal, and other interested individuals.

❖ One group of students produces a readers theatre script that is videotaped and distributed throughout the school and/or district.

❖ Several groups of students produce a readers theatre script that is videotaped and distributed throughout the school and/or district.

❖ Students join with students from another class to co-present readers theatre scripts at a grade level or all-school literacy celebration.

Suffice it to say, there is an infinite variety of presentation modes you and your students can select. It is important to share some of these options with your students and invite them to identify those with which they would be most comfortable. My rule of thumb is to "start small" at first—for example, have one or two groups of students present to the class as part of a regularly scheduled readers theatre presentation time (once a month, for example). As students gain confidence and self-assurance, they should be encouraged to take their presentations "on the road," sharing them with other classes and other grades.

INVITING AN AUDIENCE

An audience gives readers theatre legitimacy—it is a signal to students that all their hard work andpractice has a purpose: to share the fruits of their labors (and their concomitant improvements in reading fluency) with an appreciative group of individuals.

❖ Consider sending announcements or invitations to parents and other interested individuals. You may wish to design thcsc yourself or better yet, invite students to design, illustrate, and produce the invitations.

❖ In addition to parents, I have always found it appropriate (and exciting) to invite other adults with whom the students are familiar, including, for example, the school secretary, the custodian, a bus driver or two, cafeteria workers, and aides. After the presentation the students are sure to get a raft of positive comments and lots of appreciation from these individuals as they encounter them throughout the school.

❖ As appropriate, invite community members to be part of the audience. Residents of a local senior citizen center or retirement home are a most logical (and very enthusiastic) audience. These folks are always appreciative of the work of children and are often eager to see what is happening in local schools.

POST-PRESENTATION

As a wise author once said, "The play's the thing." So it is with readers theatre. In other words, the mere act of presenting a readers theatre script is complete in and of itself. It is not necessary, or even required, to do any type of formalized evaluation after readers theatre. Once again, the emphasis is on informality. Readers theatre can and should be a pleasurable and stimulating experience for children.

Following are a few ideas you may want to share with students. In doing so, you will be providing youngsters with important learning opportunities that extend and promote all aspects of your reading and language arts program.

❖ After a presentation, discuss with students how the script enhanced or altered the original story.

❖ Invite students to suggest other characters who could be added to the script.

❖ Invite students to suggest new or alternate dialogue for various characters

❖ Invite students to suggest new or different setting(s) for the script.

❖ Invite students to talk about their reactions to various characters' expressions, tone of voice, presentations, or dialogues.

❖ After a presentation, invite youngsters to suggest any modifications or changes they think could be made to the script.

PART II

This Is the Part That Comes after Part I (Which Is Why It's Called "Part II") and That Has All the Wonderfully Creative, Totally Amazing (and Sometimes Strange) Scripts You Bought This Book For

Peter, Peter (The Pumpkin-Eater) Gets Some New Stories

STAGING: There is no narrator for this story. The four characters do not have names, only numbers. They should be standing around in either a loose circle or a straight line facing the audience.

```
                    Kid 1
                     X
     Kid 2                      Kid 4
      X                          X
                    Kid 3
                     X
```

KID 1: Peter, Peter

KID 2: Pumpkin-eater,

KID 3: Had a wife . . .

KID 4: . . . and couldn't keep her.

From *MORE Tadpole Tales and Other Totally Terrific Treats for Readers Theatre* by Anthony D. Fredericks. Santa Barbara, CA: Libraries Unlimited. Copyright © 2010.

KID 1: He put her in . . .

KID 2: . . . a pumpkin shell,

KID 3: And there he kept her . . .

KID 4: . . . very well.

KID 1: Peter, Peter

KID 2: Pumpkin-eater,

KID 3: Had a wife . . .

KID 4: . . . and couldn't keep her.

KID 1: He put her in . . .

KID 2: . . . a pumpkin shell,

KID 3: And there he kept her . . .

KID 4: . . . very well.

KID 1: Peter, Peter

KID 2: Pumpkin-eater,

KID 3: Had a . . . Now wait a gosh darn minute.

KID 4: What's the matter?

KID 3: Is that it?

KID 1: What do you mean?

KID 3: Is that all we do?

KID 2: What do you mean?

KID 3: Is that the whole script? Is that all we get to say?

KID 4: Yeah, that's all we have. There isn't anything else.

KID 3: That's not much of a story.

KID 1: That's all the story there is.

KID 3: Are you sure? Are you sure there's no more story?

KID 2: That's all we have. That's all there is.

KID 3: So, all we have is a story about some guy. And the guy couldn't keep his wife. So he put his wife inside a pumpkin. And there he kept her.

KID 4: That's about it.

KID 3: That's not much of a story.

KID 1: Well, what do you suggest?

KID 3: How 'bout if Peter was a bank robber? And he put all the money inside the pumpkin.

KID 2: No, I don't think that would work.

KID 3: How 'bout if Peter was a super hero, and he saved the world from a very dangerous comet?

KID 4: No, I don't think that would work.

KID 3: How 'bout if Peter wrestled dinosaurs from a long time ago?

KID 1: No, I don't think that would work.

KID 3: Well, I give up. What can we do to make this story more exciting?

KID 2: I know, listen to this:

Peter, Peter, pumpkin-eater

Had a wife and couldn't keep her.

He put her in a pumpkin shell,

And she began to *really* smell.

KID 4: Here's another one:

Peter, Peter, pumpkin-eater

Had a wife and couldn't keep her.

He put her in a rotten pear,

And sprinkled raisins in her hair.

19

KID 1: Or how about this one:

Peter, Peter, pumpkin-eater

Had a wife and couldn't keep her.

He put her in a giant plum,

And then sat down and sucked his thumb.

KID 3: OK, I think I've got it. How about this:

Peter, Peter, pumpkin-eater

Had a wife and couldn't keep her.

He put her in a big strawberry,

It was big and very hairy.

ALL: Peter, Peter, pumpkin-eater

Had a wife and couldn't keep her.

He put her in a brand new rhyme,

And they had fun—yes, every time!

One, Two, My Face Is Blue

STAGING: The characters may be seated on chairs or stools. The narrators should be off to the side and may be at individual podiums.

		Tim	Kim	Roy	Joy
		X	X	X	X
Narrator 1	Narrator 2				
X	X				

NARRATOR 1: This is a counting story.

NARRATOR 2: We will use numbers.

NARRATOR 1: And we will use words that rhyme.

NARRATOR 2: It's a neat story.

NARRATOR 1: So listen carefully . . .

NARRATOR 2: . . . and we will tell you the story.

NARRATOR 1: Here goes.

From *MORE Tadpole Tales and Other Totally Terrific Treats for Readers Theatre* by Anthony D. Fredericks. Santa Barbara, CA: Libraries Unlimited. Copyright © 2010.

NARRATOR 2: Yeah, here goes.

TIM: One, two,

KIM: Buckle my shoe.

ROY: Three, four,

JOY: Knock at the door.

TIM: Five, six,

KIM: Pick up sticks.

ROY: Seven, eight,

JOY: Lay them straight.

TIM: Nine, ten,

KIM: A good fat hen.

NARRATOR 1: OK, let's do it again.

NARRATOR 2: But this time we'll change the words.

NARRATOR 1: Are you ready?

NARRATOR 2: Let's go!

TIM: One, two,

KIM: Eat some stew.

ROY: Three, four,

JOY: Daddy can snore.

TIM: Five, six,

KIM: My dog chews sticks.

ROY: Seven, eight,

JOY: My nose is straight.

TIM: Nine, ten,

KIM: I eat a hen.

NARRATOR 1: OK, let's do it one more time.

NARRATOR 2: And we'll change the words again.

NARRATOR 1: Are you ready?

NARRATOR 2: Let's go!

TIM: One, two,

KIM: My face is blue.

ROY: Three, four,

JOY: I sleep in a drawer.

TIM: Five, six,

KIM: My brother has ticks.

ROY: Seven, eight,

JOY: My granny can skate.

TIM: Nine, ten,

KIM: I live in a den.

NARRATOR 1: One, two,

NARRATOR 2: That's all we do.

Mary and Her Lamb Break a Rule

STAGING: All the characters may be standing or sitting on stools, except for the lamb, who may walk around while the story is being told. The narrator should be seated on a tall stool.

```
Narrator
   X
                          Mary    Lamb
                           X       X
           Mrs. Teacher
                X
                                         Billy   Sally   José
                                          X       X       X
```

NARRATOR: Mary had a little lamb,

Its fleece was white as snow.

And everywhere that Mary went,

The lamb was sure to go.

LAMB: BAAAAA, BAAAAA!

NARRATOR: It followed her to school one day,

Which was against the rule.

It made the children laugh and play

To see a lamb at school.

LAMB: BAAAAA, BAAAAA, BAAAAA!

BILLY: Hey, Mary, why did you bring your lamb to school today?

MARY: I couldn't find anybody to take care of it. Both my parents are working. And my grandmother is in Florida. I couldn't leave it at home.

SALLY: Why didn't you leave it in your yard?

MARY: It gets lonely there. Then it gets sad.

JOSÉ: Can't it play by itself?

MARY: No. It likes to be with people.

LAMB: BAAAAA, BAAAAA, BAAAAA!

MRS. TEACHER: Mary, what are you doing with that lamb at school? Don't you know the rule?

MARY: Yes, Mrs. Teacher, I know the rule. But I just couldn't leave it at home.

MRS. TEACHER: I'm sorry, Mary, but rules are rules. You won't be able to keep that lamb here. You'll have to take it right home.

MARY: Oh, please, can I keep it?

MRS. TEACHER: Mary, Mary! That's the rule

There will be no lambs in school!

This is something you must know—

Sometimes lambs just have to go!

NARRATOR: The boys and girls are working hard. They are doing math problems. Then something terrible happens. It's really, really terrible!

25

SALLY: WOW! What's that smell?

BILLY: WHEW! Does it stink in here!

JOSÉ: OOOOO-WEEEE! Let's open up the windows!

MRS. TEACHER: Mary, did your lamb just do something?

MARY: Gee, I don't know, Mrs. Teacher. [She turns to look at the lamb.] Oh, Lamby-Poo, what did you do? Oh, no, it's all over the floor.

MRS. TEACHER: [angrily] Mary, get that lamb right out of here. Clean up that floor right away. You're in big trouble, young lady. I'm going to have to call your parents.

MARY: I'm sorry, Mrs. Teacher. I'll clean it up right now. I'll never bring my lamb to school again.

NARRATOR: Mary had a little lamb,

Its fleece was white as snow.

But in the classroom one bright day,

The lamb just had to go.

LAMB: BAAAAA, BAAAAA!

NARRATOR: It made a mess upon the floor,

So bad I cannot tell.

And all the children held their nose.

They couldn't stand the smell.

LAMB: BAAAAA, BAAAAA, BAAAAA!

It's Raining, It's Pouring

STAGING: This story has no narrator. The characters should all be standing. Each one may stand at a lectern or simply holding her or his script. The "old man" may lie on a blanket on the floor in the middle of the staging area. If possible, put a blanket on a short table and invite the "old man" to lie on the table. The "old man" should be softly snoring throughout this presentation.

```
                         Teddy
                           X
        Terry                              Tommy
          X                                  X
                       "Old Man"
                           X
```

TERRY: Hey, look! [pointing to "Old Man"]

TEDDY: What?

TOMMY: It looks like an old man.

TERRY: You're right. It is an old man.

TEDDY: What is he doing here?

TOMMY: I don't know.

From *MORE Tadpole Tales and Other Totally Terrific Treats for Readers Theatre* by Anthony D. Fredericks. Santa Barbara, CA: Libraries Unlimited. Copyright © 2010.

TERRY: It looks like he's sleeping.

TEDDY: Why is he sleeping?

TOMMY: Maybe he's sleepy.

TERRY: Maybe he didn't want to go to recess.

TEDDY: Old men don't go to recess.

TOMMY: Maybe he DID go to recess, but got real tired.

TERRY: He sure can snore.

TEDDY: Yeah, he sure can.

TOMMY: He sounds like my grandmother.

TERRY: Does your grandmother snore?

TOMMY: You bet she does. She snores so loud it keeps everybody awake.

TEDDY: Wow, she's a loud snorer.

TERRY: Just like our friend. [points to "Old Man"]

TOMMY: Why does he snore all the time?

TEDDY: Maybe he swallowed a fly.

TERRY: Or maybe he ate an elephant.

TOMMY: AN ELEPHANT! How could he swallow an elephant?

TERRY: My dad eats stuff all the time.

TEDDY: Does your dad eat elephants?

TERRY: No. But one time he said he was so hungry that he could eat a horse.

TOMMY: So, your father eats horses?

TERRY: I don't think so, but he sure does eat a lot!

TEDDY: Maybe our friend here [points to "Old Man"] bumped his head.

TOMMY: Why?

28

TEDDY: Well, I bumped my head once.

TERRY: Did it make you snore?

TEDDY: No, I don't think so. But it sure did hurt.

TOMMY: Maybe old people snore when they hit their heads.

TERRY: Maybe they do. Old people do funny things.

TEDDY: Yeah, like Tommy's grandmother.

TOMMY: You mean my snoring grandmother!

TERRY: Well, what do we do now?

TEDDY: Well, maybe we can sing a song.

TOMMY: I like to sing!

TERRY: So do I.

TEDDY: Then let's sing a song about our snoring friend here.

TOMMY: OK.

TERRY: OK.

TEDDY: Here we go. It's raining,

TOMMY: It's pouring,

TERRY: The old man is snoring.

TEDDY: He went to bed

TOMMY: And bumped his head

TERRY: And couldn't get up in the morning.

TEDDY: If he couldn't get up in the morning then he couldn't go to recess.

TOMMY: Poor old man.

TERRY: Poor old man

TEDDY: Poor old snoring man.

ALL: Bye, bye, old man. [They all exit the staging area.]

After students have presented this script, invite the entire class to participate in the following song. (A musical rendition of this song can be found at http://kids.niehs.nih.gov/lyrics/itsraining.htm.) Have students stand in a large circle. As each line of the song is sung, students may perform selected actions with their hands and other body parts.

❖ It's raining, it's pouring [Students all raise their arms in the air and wiggle their fingers.]

❖ The old man is snoring [Students clasp their hands together and put them on one side of their heads as though they are sleeping—snoring sounds are optional.]

❖ He went to bed [Students reach down to the floor and pull an imaginary blanket up over their heads.]

❖ And bumped his head [Students tap their foreheads lightly with their fists.]

❖ And couldn't get up in the morning [Students raise their arms again and let out some loud yawns.]

A Bunch of Mice on a Clock

STAGING: The narrator may stand or sit off to the side. The characters may be seated on stools or standing.

Narrator				
X				
	Mouse 1	Mouse 2	Mouse 3	
	X	X	X	
				Clock
				X

NARRATOR: Once upon a time there were three mice. They did not have names. They were called Mouse 1, Mouse 2, and Mouse 3. They were strange. One day they wanted to know what time it was. I don't know why. They just wanted to know. So they ran around the house. They ran up the stairs. They ran down the stairs. Then they saw a tall clock. It was in the living room.

MOUSE 1: Look, a tall clock!

From *MORE Tadpole Tales and Other Totally Terrific Treats for Readers Theatre* by Anthony D. Fredericks. Santa Barbara, CA: Libraries Unlimited. Copyright © 2010.

MOUSE 2: Yes, look, a tall clock!

MOUSE 3: That's what he said.

MOUSE 2: Yes, I know.

MOUSE 3: So now what?

MOUSE 1: Let's run up the clock.

MOUSE 2: Why?

MOUSE 1: That is what mice do.

MOUSE 2: They do?

MOUSE 3: Yes, we do!

NARRATOR: So the mice ran up the clock.

CLOCK: Hey, stop that. That tickles!

MOUSE 1: We just want to know what time it is.

MOUSE 2: Yes. We just want to know what time it is!

MOUSE 3: Yes, what they said. [points to Mouse 1 and Mouse 2]

CLOCK: Why don't you get a watch?

MOUSE 1: Are you kidding? If you look real hard, you'll see that I don't have any arms. How would I wear a watch?

MOUSE 2: Yes, how would we wear a watch?

MOUSE 3: Yes, what they said.

CLOCK: Why don't you buy an alarm clock?

MOUSE 1: Because we are mice! We don't have any money.

MOUSE 2: Yes, we don't have any money!

MOUSE 3: Yes, what they said. [points to Mouse 1 and Mouse 2]

CLOCK: What about the clock in your kitchen?

MOUSE 1: What kitchen?

MOUSE 2: Yes, what kitchen?

MOUSE 3: Yes, what kitchen?

CLOCK: Oh, that's right! You are mice . . .

MOUSE 1: . . . and we don't have a kitchen.

MOUSE 2: . . . yes, and we don't have a kitchen.

MOUSE 3: . . . yes, what they said. [points to Mouse 1 and Mouse 2]

CLOCK: Well, I can't help you.

MOUSE 1: Why not?

MOUSE 2: Yes, why not?

MOUSE 3: Yes, what they said. [points to Mouse 1 and Mouse 2]

CLOCK: Because when you walk on me I want to giggle. I want to laugh. I want to giggle and laugh.

MOUSE 1: Why is that?

MOUSE 2: Yes, why is that?

MOUSE 3: Yes, what they said. [points to Mouse 1 and Mouse 2]

CLOCK: Because I am ticklish. When you walk on me I get ticklish. I want to laugh. I want to giggle. I want to laugh and giggle.

MOUSE 1: You are a strange clock!

MOUSE 2: Yes, you are a strange clock.

MOUSE 3: Yes, what they said. [points to Mouse 1 and Mouse 2]

MOUSE 1: Hey, I have an idea!

MOUSE 2: Hey, he has an idea!

MOUSE 3: Hey, what is your idea?

MOUSE 1: Let's run all over the clock. Let's make him laugh. Let's make him giggle.

MOUSE 2: Hey, that's a good idea!

MOUSE 3: Yes, what he said. [points to Mouse 2]

NARRATOR: So the mice run all over the clock. They run up the clock. They run down the clock. They run all over the clock.

CLOCK: Ha, ha, ha, hee, hee, hee, ho, ho.

NARRATOR: The mice keep running. They keep running all over the clock.

CLOCK: Ha, ha, ha, hee, hee, hee, ho, ho, ho. Ha, ha, ha, hee, hee, hee, ho, ho, ho. Stop it! Stop it! Stop it!

NARRATOR: The mice tickle the clock some more.

CLOCK: Ha, ha, ha, hee, hee, hee, ho, ho, ho. Ha, ha, ha, hee, hee, hee, ho, ho, ho. Stop it! Stop it! Stop it!

MOUSE 1: Gee, this is fun!

MOUSE 2: Yes, this is fun!

MOUSE 3: Yes, what he said. [points to Mouse 2]

NARRATOR: So the mice ran all over the clock. They ran up the clock. They ran down the clock. They ran all over the clock. The clock laughed. The clock giggled. The clock laughed and giggled.

MOUSE 1: [to audience] And you know what?

MOUSE 2: No, what?

MOUSE 3: Yes, what he said. [points to Mouse 2]

MOUSE 1: [pointing to audience] If you are ticklish, we'll run all over you.

MOUSE 2: Yes, we'll run all over you.

MOUSE 3: Yes, what they said. [points to Mouse 2 and Mouse 3]

MOUSE 1: [pointing to audience] And you will laugh and giggle.

MOUSE 2: [pointing to audience] Yes, you will laugh and giggle.

MOUSE 3: [pointing to Mouse 2 and Mouse 3] Yes, what they said.

ALL MICE: Ha, ha, ha, hee, hee, hee, ho, ho, ho.

Ha, ha, ha, hee, hee, hee, ho, ho, ho.

Ha, ha, ha, hee, hee, hee, ho, ho, ho.

Ha, ha, ha, hee, hee, hee, ho, ho, ho.

Three Squirrels + One Bad Pig

STAGING: The narrator sits on a tall stool. The three squirrels and the pig should be standing.

```
                        Third Squirrel
                              X


                        Second Squirrel
                              X

                         First Squirrel
                              X
                                          Big Bad Pig
                                              X
        Narrator
           X
```

NARRATOR: You've heard the story about the three little pigs. But have you ever heard the story about the three little squirrels? Well, in this story the three little squirrels leave home and begin walking in the woods. Then something really terrible happens.

FIRST SQUIRREL: Hey, brothers, it looks like we're lost.

SECOND SQUIRREL:	You're right. I guess we better all build a house for the night.
THIRD SQUIRREL:	OK, let's get started.
NARRATOR:	Each of the squirrels goes off to hunt for materials. Now, you should know that these three little squirrels are not as smart as your everyday average squirrel. In fact, they're pretty dumb. Listen, and you'll see for yourself.
FIRST SQUIRREL:	I'm going to build a three-story house out of these weeds I found by the river.
SECOND SQUIRREL:	Are you crazy? Do you know what can happen? A big bad pig could just come along and blow your house down.
THIRD SQUIRREL:	Well, brother, what are you going to use to build your house?
SECOND SQUIRREL:	I found thousands and thousands of dried leaves in the forest. I'm going to build an enormous house with these materials.
FIRST SQUIRREL:	You know, you must be just as crazy as I am. Don't you know that that big, ugly, terrible pig with bad breath could just as easily come along and blow your house down, too?
SECOND SQUIRREL:	Gosh, maybe you're right. [turning to the Third Squirrel] What are you going to do, brother?
THIRD SQUIRREL:	I think I'm going to get out of these woods and move to a big apartment building in the city. That will keep that big, lard-faced, funny-nosed, overweight porker from blowing down my house. How would you guys like to move in with me?
FIRST SQUIRREL:	Sounds good to me.
SECOND SQUIRREL:	Me, too!
BIG BAD PIG:	Hey, just wait a minute. This isn't how the story is supposed to turn out.

NARRATOR: [standing up] Well, guess what, pork breath? We just decided to change this story right in the middle. I guess you're left out.

FIRST SQUIRREL: Yeah, you're left out!

SECOND SQUIRREL: Yeah, you're outta here!

THIRD SQUIRREL: [waving] Bye, bye!

BIG BAD PIG: Well, now what am I supposed to do?

NARRATOR: I guess you'll just have to find yourself another story. Why don't you go over to Little Red Riding Hood's house? Maybe she and her granny will invite you over for dinner. Maybe they'll even have YOU for dinner. Yum yum, pork chops for dinner with lots and lots of gravy and lots and lots of mashed potatoes and lots and lots of coconut custard pie. YUM, YUM! Maybe we'll even have you for dinner. Doesn't that sound good, boys?

FIRST SQUIRREL: YEAH! That does sound good.

SECOND SQUIRREL: It sounds really good! UMMMMMMMMMMMM!

THIRD SQUIRREL: IT SOUNDS REALLY, REALLY GOOD!! YUMMMMMMMMMM!

BIG BAD PIG: Hey, stop looking at me that way you guys. [backing away] This isn't the way the story is supposed to turn out. [frantic] The writer was supposed to make me big and bad, not the other way around. [more frantic] Anyway, what did I ever do to you guys? [backing away as the Narrator and the three wolves begin approaching]

FIRST SQUIRREL: [licking lips] YUMMMMMM!.

SECOND SQUIRREL: [rubbing hands together] YUMMMMMM! YUMMMMMM!

THIRD SQUIRREL: [wild-eyed] YUMMY! YUMMY! YUMMY!

BIG BAD PIG: [very frantic] Hey, you guys, just get away. Now stop it! No, no, no!!! [exits rapidly with the others in pursuit]

38

Little Bo-Peep Forgets a Lot of Stuff

STAGING: The narrator stands behind or to the side of the characters. The characters may be standing or seated on tall stools.

Narrator X			
	Bo-Peep X	Clarence X	Sheep X
Mr. Smart X			
Penny X			

NARRATOR: Once upon a time there was this little girl named Bo-Peep. She was a nice girl and everybody liked her. But she had this problem. She was always losing things.

MR. SMART: Alright kids, I want everyone to take out their homework from last night.

From *MORE Tadpole Tales and Other Totally Terrific Treats for Readers Theatre* by Anthony D. Fredericks. Santa Barbara, CA: Libraries Unlimited. Copyright © 2010.

BO-PEEP: [raising her hand] Mr. Smart, I guess I forgot my homework. I left it on the kitchen table this morning.

MR. SMART: [exasperated] Oh, not again, Bo-Peep. That's the third time this week you've forgotten your homework. What are we going to do with you?

BO-PEEP: I'm sorry, Mr. Smart. I just can't remember anything. Just last week I forgot my sheep.

SHEEP: BAAAAA, BAAAAA, BAAAAA!

MR. SMART: What do you mean, you forgot your sheep?

BO-PEEP: Well, you see it was like this. I was at the park with my friends. And I had my sheep with me, because I'm supposed to watch him all the time. Well, we were having so much fun that I forgot all about my sheep. And when it was time to go home he was gone. We looked everywhere and couldn't find him.

PENNY: Yeah, that's right. I was there. We looked everywhere. We looked in the trees. We looked in the bushes. We even looked on the jungle gym and in the sandbox. But he was gone.

SHEEP: BAAAAA, BAAAAA, BAAAAA!

BO-PEEP: Yeah, and just a couple of days ago I lost my library book. It just vanished out of my desk.

MR. SMART: Can't you hold on to anything?

BO-PEEP: It just seems that everything I touch seems to vanish.

MR. SMART: What are we going to do with you?

CLARENCE: I know. Why don't we tie a string around her finger or something like that?

PENNY: Maybe we could write a note. And maybe we could put the note in Bo-Peep's pocket.

BO-PEEP: But what if I leave the note in my pocket? What if my mother washes my shirt with the note in it?

CLARENCE: Hmmm. I guess that won't work.

SHEEP: BAAAAA, BAAAAA, BAAAAA!

MR. SMART: How can we help Bo-Peep to remember things?

CLARENCE: Why don't we put the sheep in her pocket?

SHEEP: BAAAAA, BAAAAA, BAAAAA!

PENNY: No, I don't think that would work.

CLARENCE: Why don't we tie the sheep around her finger?

SHEEP: BAAAAA, BAAAAA, BAAAAA!

PENNY: No, I don't think that will work either.

CLARENCE: [very excited] I know, I know! Maybe the sheep has a good memory. Maybe the sheep could remember.

PENNY: I think you're right!

MR. SMART: I think you have a good idea, Clarence.

PENNY: I think you have a great idea.

SHEEP: BAAAAA, BAAAAA, BAAAAA!

NARRATOR: And so it was! Every day the sheep came to school. Every day the sheep learned about math. Every day the sheep learned to read. Every day the sheep went to recess and to the library. Every day the sheep got on the bus and got off the bus.

CLARENCE: Don't forget about Bo-Peep!

PENNY: Yeah, don't forget about Bo-Peep!

NARRATOR: That's right! Every day the sheep brought Bo-Peep to school. Bo-Peep didn't have to remember anything. The sheep always remembered. And the sheep lived happily ever after! And so did Bo-Peep!

SHEEP: BAAAAA, BAAAAA, BAAAAA!

Hey Diddle, Diddle

STAGING: The narrator stands behind or to the side of the characters. The characters may be standing or seated on tall stools.

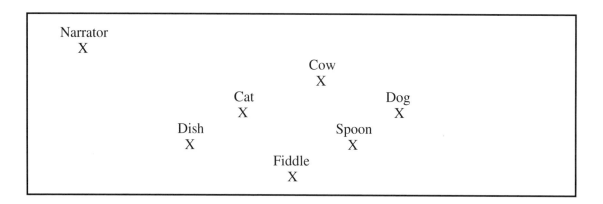

NARRATOR: Hey, diddle, diddle,

The cat and the fiddle,

The cow jumped

Over the moon.

The little dog laughed

To see such sport,

And the dish ran away

With the spoon.

COW: You know what? This is a pretty good story.

CAT: Why do you say that?

COW: Well, because I get to jump over the moon.

DOG: Tell me something—how do you do that?

COW: Well, I guess it's because I'm really, really strong.

DISH: You must be. I don't think I've ever seen a cow jump that high before.

SPOON: You know what, I haven't either!

COW: Well, you see it's this way. I went to my doctor and she said I had to exercise more. I was pretty weak and she gave me some really good exercises that would make me strong.

FIDDLE: You must have done a lot of exercising. I don't think I could jump as high as you can.

CAT: I don't think I could jump that high either.

DOG: Hey, you know, you [points to Cat] still can jump pretty high. I've watched you before.

DISH: That's right. Cat is one of the best jumpers in the neighborhood.

SPOON: Yeah, I've seen him jump really high many times.

FIDDLE: But you know something, in this story Cat doesn't get to jump.

COW: That's right, he doesn't get to jump at all.

CAT: Yes, it's just me and my friend Fiddle, who just sing our way through this story.

DOG: You're absolutely right. You spend the entire story just singing "Hey, diddle, diddle" over and over again.

43

DISH: You know what—I wish I could sing like Cat and the Fiddle.

SPOON: Well, you know, there's one thing you can do.

FIDDLE: That's right. You two [points to Dish and Spoon] get to run away. It's not much, but it is an important part of the story.

COW: But I want to know where the two of you go when you run away.

CAT: Yeah, where do you two go in such a hurry?

DISH: To be honest with you, I really don't know.

SPOON: I don't know, either. The person who wrote the story didn't tell us where we were supposed to run to. They just told us to run away.

DOG: Maybe the two of you ran over to another story—you know, one of those stories about three little pigs or one of those stories about a girl with a red riding hood or maybe a story about an old lady who lived in an old smelly shoe.

DISH: Yeah, maybe we did.

SPOON: And then again, maybe we didn't.

CAT: Hey, let's not forget our friend here. [points to Dog] He has a part in this little story, too, don't forget.

FIDDLE: You're right. Our friend gets to laugh during the whole story. Yeah, that's all he does—laugh, laugh, laugh.

DOG: Ha, ha, ha!

COW: I guess the writers made him do all that laughing because this is a really funny story.

CAT: Yes, it is. Look at all the funny things we do.

DISH: We do funny things . . .

SPOON: . . . and silly things . . .

FIDDLE: . . . and strange things!

COW: I guess that's why this is such a great story.

ALL: YEAH!!!

NARRATOR: Hey, diddle, diddle,
The cat and the fiddle,
The cow jumped
Over the moon.
The little dog laughed
To see such sport,
And the dish ran away
With the spoon.

DOG: Ha, ha, ha!

The Boy in Blue

STAGING: The characters may all be seated on stools. "Little Boy Blue" (who has a nonspeaking role) may be lying on the floor, pretending to be asleep.

Alice	Alex	Abby	Anna		Little Boy Blue
X	X	X	X		X
				Narrator	
				X	

NARRATOR: Welcome to our story.

ALICE: It's a fun story.

ALEX: It's a story about a boy.

ABBY: A boy all dressed in blue.

ANNA: Why is he in blue?

ALICE: Maybe he likes blue.

ALEX: I like blue.

ABBY: I like blue, too.

ANNA: Well, so do I.

ALICE: I guess we all like blue.

NARRATOR: There's something else they [points to audience] need to know.

ALEX: What's that?

NARRATOR: Well, our blue boy lives on a farm.

ABBY: How do you know that?

NARRATOR: Well. I'm the narrator. I'm supposed to know everything.

ANNA: Oh, now I get it. You're the narrator because you know a lot of stuff.

NARRATOR: Well, not really! I just know a lot of stuff about this story.

ALICE: Like the boy all dressed in blue.

NARRATOR: Yes.

ALEX: And the fact that he lives on a farm.

NARRATOR: That's right.

ABBY: So, does that mean we can start the story?

NARRATOR: I guess so. Is everybody ready?

ANNA: I think we are.

NARRATOR: All right. Ladies and gentlemen, we now present the story about a little boy. He was all dressed in blue. And he lived on a farm. Let's go!

ALICE: Little boy blue,

ALEX: Come, blow your horn.

ABBY: The sheep's in the meadow,

ANNA: The cow's in the corn.

ALICE: Where's the little boy?

ALEX: Who looks after the sheep?

ABBY: [points to Little Boy Blue] He's under the haystack,

ANNA: Fast asleep.

NARRATOR: That was a good story. You did a good job.

ALICE: I'm tired from that story.

ALEX: So am I.

ABBY: I'm tired, too.

ANNA: And so am I.

[The four main characters get off their stools/chairs and go over to Little Boy Blue. They all lie down on the floor and pretend to go to sleep. They may begin snoring quietly.]

NARRATOR: Well, our story's done. Everybody worked hard.
Now they are all tired. Good night, everyone.

On Top of Spaghetti

STAGING: The characters may all be seated on chairs or stools. The narrator may be off to the side standing at a lectern or music stand. You may wish to play the music to this ever-popular camp song for background or so students can sing their lines along with the music. A midi file of the song can be found at http://kids.niehs.nih.gov/lyrics/ontopofspag.htm.

```
                                                    Narrator
                                                       X
                                          Chad
    Enrique                                 X
       X
              Sarah             Ben
                X                X
```

NARRATOR: Once upon a time there were four students. They all worked very hard. They learned how to read. They learned how to add numbers. They learned all about animals. They were very smart students. But that hard work made them hungry.

SARAH: Boy, am I hungry!

ENRIQUE: Yeah, I'm hungry, too!

CHAD: You know, this learning makes me hungry!

BEN: Me, too.

SARAH: I wonder when lunch will be.

ENRIQUE: I don't know if I can wait.

BEN: I hope it comes soon. I'm starving.

CHAD: So am I.

ENRIQUE: Does anybody know what we're having?

BEN: I wasn't listening to the morning announcements.

SARAH: Neither was I.

CHAD: I hope it's something good.

SARAH: Me too.

CHAD: I think we're having spaghetti?

ENRIQUE: Spaghetti! UMMMMM! I love spaghetti.

SARAH: I like spaghetti better than hamburgers.

CHAD: I like spaghetti better than peanut butter sandwiches.

BEN: I love spaghetti better than anything.

CHAD: You mean, better than ice cream?

BEN: Welllllll, maybe not as much as ice cream.

CHAD: How about spaghetti with ice cream on top?

SARAH: Ohhhhh, gross!

ENRIQUE: Yeah, that's really gross.

BEN: Hey, I have an idea.

SARAH: What's that?

BEN: Why don't we write a song about spaghetti?

ENRIQUE: Hey, that sounds great! I mean, we're really smart. Writing a song should be fun.

SARAH: So, what do we do?

BEN: Let's think of something funny. A funny song about spaghetti would be fun.

ALL: OK.

NARRATOR: And so the students began to write. They wrote a song about spaghetti. They wrote a funny song about spaghetti. They worked really hard. They would like to sing it for you, so listen carefully. Their song is called "On Top of Spaghetti." Are you ready? Here goes.

SARAH: On top of spaghetti,

ENRIQUE: All covered with cheese,

CHAD: I lost my poor meatball

BEN: When somebody sneezed.

SARAH: It rolled off the table,

ENRIQUE: And onto the floor,

CHAD: And then my poor meatball

BEN: Rolled out of the door.

SARAH: It rolled into the garden,

ENRIQUE: And under a bush,

CHAD: And then my poor meatball

BEN: Was nothing but mush!

SARAH: The mush was as tasty,

ENRIQUE: As tasty could be,

CHAD: And then the next summer ,

BEN: It grew into a tree.

SARAH: The tree was all covered,

ENRIQUE: All covered with moss.

CHAD: And on it grew meatballs,

51

BEN: All covered with sauce.

SARAH: So if you have spaghetti,

ENRIQUE: All covered with cheese,

CHAD: Hold onto your meatball,

BEN: 'Cause someone might sneeze.

[Invite students to repeat the script (as below) while playing a recording of the music in the background (if possible). They may wish to add the accompanying hand movements to this second version of the script.]

SARAH: On top of spaghetti, [point to center of circle]

ENRIQUE: All covered with cheese, [pretend to shake parmesan cheese]

CHAD: I lost my poor meatball [hunch shoulders and shake head]

BEN: When somebody sneezed. [simulate sneezing; cover mouth with hand]

SARAH: It rolled off the table, [roll both hands over and over]

ENRIQUE: And onto the floor, [point to the floor]

CHAD: And then my poor meatball [hands together in round shape]

BEN: Rolled out of the door. [roll both hands over and over]

SARAH: It rolled into the garden, [roll both hands over and over]

ENRIQUE: And under a bush, [bend over and point to the left]

CHAD: And then my poor meatball [hands together in round shape]

BEN: Was nothing but mush! [wiggle fingers all around]

SARAH: The mush was as tasty, [simulate eating with a fork]

ENRIQUE: As tasty could be, [lick lips]

CHAD: And then the next summer, [wipe brow with one hand]

BEN: It grew into a tree. [hands together and move from floor upward]

SARAH: The tree was all covered, [move hands all around]

ENRIQUE: All covered with moss. [hold nose]

CHAD: And on it grew meatballs, [hands together in round shape]

BEN: All covered with sauce. [simulate pouring a jar of sauce]

SARAH: So if you have spaghetti, [point to center of circle]

ENRIQUE: All covered with cheese, [pretend to shake parmesan cheese]

CHAD: Hold onto your meatball, [hold hands together]

BEN: 'Cause someone might sneeze. [simulate sneezing; cover mouth with hand]

NARRATOR: And that's the end of their story. Now, let's go get some lunch!

Round and Round and Round and Round

STAGING: Throughout the story the narrator walks in a continuous circle around the other characters. The other characters may all be seated or standing. They should occasionally turn their heads, looking at the narrator while speaking their parts.

```
                          Kim
                           X
          Narrator              Ken        Karen
             X                   X           X
                          Kyle
                           X
```

NARRATOR: Here we go round the mulberry bush,
The mulberry bush, the mulberry bush.
Here we go round the mulberry bush,
So early in the . . .
WHOA, now wait a minute here. Why am I walking around in circles?

KIM: I guess it's because you're the hero of this story.

NARRATOR: If I'm the hero, then I'm one very dizzy hero.

KAREN: To be honest, I think you were pretty dizzy to begin with.

NARRATOR: Hey, who are you calling dizzy?

KYLE: Hold on, guys. I think there's a real problem here.

KEN: What do you mean?

KYLE: Well, just look at our friendly narrator. Ever since this story began, all he's been doing is walking around in circles.

NARRATOR: I can't help it. The writer wanted me to go around and around some silly mulberry bush. The only problem is, I have no idea what a mulberry bush is or what one looks like. [NOTE: During the following conversation the narrator continues to circle the other characters.]

KIM: Don't look at me. I've never seen one, either.

KAREN: I think I saw one in another story. But I'm not quite sure.

KEN: What other story would that be?

KAREN: I can't remember. I think it had something to do with some pigs and a squirrel with bad breath.

KYLE: No, it wasn't that story.

KIM: I think it was the one about the cow who wanted to jump over the moon.

KAREN: No, it can't be that one.

KYLE: What about the story with the old lady who lived in a shoe?

KEN: No, not that one!

KAREN: I think it was the story about the little girl who brought that lamb to school one day and then the lamb did something really gross on the floor of the

55

classroom and then the teacher had to stop in the middle of her lesson to get some paper towels and clean it . . .

NARRATOR: HOLD IT! HOLD IT! Now wait just a gosh darn minute here. While you guys are talking about Mother Goose and all her crazy characters, I'm still going around and around in circles here—and there's not even a stupid mulberry bush for miles. Can't anybody stop me?

KEN: No, not me!

KYLE: Not me, either!

KAREN: No, I can't!

KIM: I guess not.

KEN: Hey, guys, it looks like our friendly Narrator is going to have to solve this problem alone.

KYLE: Hey, let's see if we can find a story where the Narrator isn't going around and around.

KIM: Great idea!

KAREN: Yeah, let's go. [All the characters get up and begin to leave.]

NARRATOR: Hey, guys, wait up. You're not just going to leave me here. Hey, wait. Wait. Hey . . . [The narrator continues to go around in circles as his or her voice trails off.]

Peter Piper and His Pickled Peppers

STAGING: The four players should be seated on chairs or tall stools. The narrator should be standing. Note that the audience has a small part at the end.

Larry	Lincoln	Laura	LaToya	
X	X	X	X	
				Narrator
				X

NARRATOR: Hi, folks. We have an exciting readers theatre for you today. Our four players [points to the four players] will share a popular Mother Goose rhyme with you. But this is a tricky story. That's because there are many words in the story that begin with the same letter. That makes them hard to say. In fact, almost all the words start with the letter "P." So let's listen carefully and see how they do.

LARRY: Hey, don't forget about their part. [points to audience]

From *MORE Tadpole Tales and Other Totally Terrific Treats for Readers Theatre* by Anthony D. Fredericks. Santa Barbara, CA: Libraries Unlimited. Copyright © 2010.

NARRATOR: Thanks, I almost DID forget. We have a part for you [points to audience] in this script. When I point to you, all of you will say "Peter Piper picked a peck of pickled peppers; a peck of pickled peppers Peter Piper picked." Here is what you will say, again—"Peter Piper picked a peck of pickled peppers; a peck of pickled peppers Peter Piper picked." OK? Are you ready, players? [points to players]

ALL PLAYERS: Yes.

NARRATOR: Are you ready, audience? [points to audience]

AUDIENCE: Yes.

NARRATOR: Then, let's go. Larry, start us off.

LARRY: Peter Piper

LINCOLN: picked a peck

LAURA: of pickled . . .

LATOYA: peppers;

LARRY: A peck

LINCOLN: of pickled peppers

LAURA: Peter Piper

LATOYA: picked.

LARRY: If Peter Piper

LINCOLN: picked a peck

LAURA: of pickled

LATOYA: peppers,

LARRY: Where's

LINCOLN: the peck

LAURA: of pickled

LATOYA: peppers

LARRY: Peter

LINCOLN: Piper

LAURA: picked?

[The Narrator points to the audience.]

AUDIENCE: Peter Piper picked a peck of pickled peppers; a peck of pickled peppers Peter Piper picked.

NARRATOR: OK, very good. Now, let's do it again. But this time we'll do it really, really fast. Are you ready? OK, let's go!

[The players will read their parts at a much faster clip than in the first round. (Be prepared for lots of giggling!)]

LARRY: Peter Piper

LINCOLN: picked a peck

LAURA: of pickled . . .

LATOYA: peppers;

LARRY: A peck

LINCOLN: of pickled peppers

LAURA: Peter Piper

LATOYA: picked.

LARRY: If Peter Piper

LINCOLN: picked a peck

LAURA: of pickled

LATOYA: peppers,

LARRY: Where's

LINCOLN: the peck

LAURA: of pickled

LATOYA: peppers

LARRY: Peter

LINCOLN: Piper

LAURA: picked?

[The Narrator points to the audience.]

AUDIENCE: Peter Piper picked a peck of pickled peppers; a peck of pickled peppers Peter Piper picked.

[As appropriate, invite the players to repeat their parts at an extremely rapid pace, as fast as they can. Watch out for lots of laughs!.]

NARRATOR: Congratulations. You did a great job.

Little Red Riding Hood's New Adventure

STAGING: The characters may stand at podiums or music stands. The Squirrel and Red Riding Hood may wish to "walk" over to Granny and the Hunter for the later parts of the production. The narrator should be standing off to the side for the entire production.

	Red Riding Hood X	Squirrel X		
Narrator X			Granny X	Hunter X

NARRATOR: Once upon a time there lived a little girl by the name of Little Red Riding Hood. One day she decided to visit her dear old grandmother, who lived on the other side of the woods.

LITTLE RED RIDING HOOD: I haven't seen my dear old granny for quite some time. I think that I shall take her a basket of treats.

NARRATOR: The woods were very dangerous and there were lots of creatures that lived in the woods—like wolves and bears and especially squirrels. But Red Riding Hood decided it was a good idea to see her grandmother. She just hoped that she wouldn't see any wolves or bears or squirrels in the woods.

So she set out with her basket. She walked through the woods and before long a very large squirrel jumped out from behind a tree.

SQUIRREL: Good day, Little Red Riding Hood. Where are you off to?

LITTLE RED RIDING HOOD: I am off to see my dear old grandmother, who lives on the other side of the woods. I am bringing her some treats and we shall have a picnic. And by the way, how can a squirrel talk?

SQUIRREL: Hey, didn't you know?—this is a fairy tale. Anyway, what kinds of treats do you have? I love treats!

LITTLE RED RIDING HOOD: Well, I have some yogurt. And I have some chocolate chip cookies. And I have some banana cream pie. And I have some nuts.

NARRATOR: As soon as the squirrel heard the word "nuts" his ears started to quiver and he started to drool.

SQUIRREL: Hmmm, nuts! That's very interesting. Well, I hope you are safe and that you take your time as you walk in the woods.

NARRATOR: Little Red Riding Hood continued down the trail. Meanwhile the squirrel, who really liked his nuts, decided that he could have some fun. So he scampered through the woods and arrived at grandmother's house long before Little Red Riding Hood. He knocked on the door.

GRANNY: Who's there?

SQUIRREL:	It's just me. I am lost and hope that you might be able to help me with some directions.
GRANNY:	Very well. I shall be glad to help you with some directions.
NARRATOR:	With that, Granny opened the door. Before she knew it, the squirrel punched her right in the nose. Granny fell right on the floor. The squirrel quickly grabbed her by her pajamas and dragged her into the closet. Then he quickly slipped into Granny's other pajamas and jumped into her bed. Before long Little Red Riding Hood arrived at the house and knocked on the door.
SQUIRREL:	[in a high-pitched voice] Who's there?
LITTLE RED RIDING HOOD:	It's me, Granny. I have a basket filled with yogurt and cookies and pie and some nuts. I thought you might like to have a picnic.
SQUIRREL:	[in a high-pitched voice] Well, why didn't you say so? Come right in.
NARRATOR:	And so Little Red Riding Hood entered the house. And there in the bed was the squirrel dressed up in Granny's pajamas.
LITTLE RED RIDING HOOD:	My, Granny, what funny ears you have.
SQUIRREL:	The better to listen to you, my dear.
LITTLE RED RIDING HOOD:	My, Granny, what strange eyes you have.
SQUIRREL:	The better to see you, my dear.
LITTLE RED RIDING HOOD:	My, Granny, what big front teeth you have.
GRANNY:	The better to eat up all your nuts, my dear.
NARRATOR:	With that the squirrel jumped out of the bed and grabbed the basket from Little Red Riding Hood. He

pawed and pawed his way through the basket until he found the nuts at the bottom. He grabbed all the nuts and stuffed them in his mouth. [At this point the "Squirrel" may puff up his or her cheeks.] As he was stuffing his cheeks, Little Red Riding Hood let out a little, tiny scream. A nearby hunter heard the little, tiny scream and ran to the house.

HUNTER: Hey, what was that little, tiny scream?

NARRATOR: Just as the hunter entered the house he saw the squirrel all dressed up in Granny's pajamas with his cheeks full of nuts. Right away he knew what had happened.

HUNTER: Hey, everybody, it looks like you're having a picnic. Can I come, too?

LITTLE RED RIDING HOOD: Sure you can. But first you have to help me find my dear old grandmother. I don't know where she is.

NARRATOR: And so the hunter and Little Red Riding Hood began looking all over the house. Before long they found Granny in the bedroom closet. By now she was awake

GRANNY: You saved me! You saved me from that horrible squirrel. Thank you very much.

HUNTER: I'm glad I could save you from the squirrel.

NARRATOR: After that, Little Red Riding Hood, the hunter, and the dear old grandmother went to McDonald's to have some burgers and fries and chocolate milk shakes. And the squirrel. . .well, I guess the squirrel is still feeding his face with all those nuts back at Granny's place.

The Old Woman and All Those Kids

STAGING: The narrator stands behind and to the side of the other characters. The other characters may stand or sit on high stools.

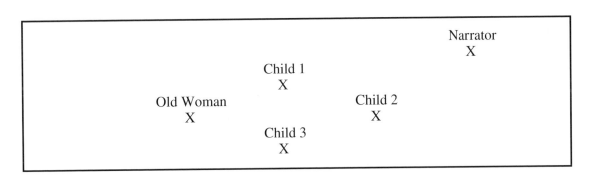

NARRATOR: Once upon a time there was an old woman who lived in a shoe.

OLD WOMAN: Hey, how come I have to live in a shoe?

NARRATOR: I don't know, lady. I'm just here to tell the story.

OLD WOMAN: Yeah, but I don't want to live in a shoe.

NARRATOR: Sorry, I can't help you. I'm just reading what the author put here in the script.

OLD WOMAN: [angry] Well, that author person sure must be stupid. Why the heck would he put an old lady like me into an old shoe like this? He must really be stupid, stupid, stupid!

NARRATOR: Hey, don't blame me. I was just hired to tell this story. I tell the story, I get my money, and then I'm outta here. I'm just doin' my job lady.

OLD WOMAN: [exasperated] Well, OK, but let's get this over with, OK?

NARRATOR: OK. Anyway, as I was saying . . . . Once upon a time there was an old woman who lived in a shoe. She had so many children, she didn't know what to do.

OLD WOMAN: Now just a gosh darn minute here. First you have me living in an old shoe . . .

NARRATOR: Right.

OLD WOMAN: Then you give me about 24 children . . .

NARRATOR: That's what I said . . .

OLD WOMAN: So where the heck did all these children come from? It's like I'm living with a whole classroom full of kids.

NARRATOR: Like I said, I'm just doing my job lady. I just read what it says here. And it says that you had a whole bunch of children.

OLD WOMAN: But I don't want a whole bunch of children. I just want to live alone in peace and quiet.

NARRATOR: But you can't live alone.

OLD WOMAN: Why's that?

NARRATOR: 'Cause the author person says that you had so many children you didn't know what to do.

OLD WOMAN: [angry] Hey, I know what I'm going to do to that stupid author person. I'm going to take him by his skinny little neck and I'm going to . . . .

NARRATOR: Hey, let's not get violent here. Remember, this is a children's story, and we can't have any violence in a children's story.

OLD WOMAN: [exasperated] Well, OK, if you say so. I just better not catch that author person hanging around my neighborhood any time soon.

NARRATOR: Can I get on with the story?

OLD WOMAN: Yeah, go ahead!

NARRATOR: Well, according to what I was paid to read it says here [points to script] that . . . there was an old woman who lived in a shoe, she had so many children she didn't know what to do, she gave them some broth without any bread, then whipped them all soundly and put them to bed.

CHILD 1: Whoa! Just a minute there. What kind of old woman is this? [points to Old Woman]

CHILD 2: Yeah, what he/she said. [points to Child 1]

CHILD 3: Yeah, you mean this old woman has a whole bunch of kids running around all over the place, and she can't even feed them?

NARRATOR: I'm just reading my script. Don't look at me!

CHILD 1: Yeah, and then she goes and gives them all some warm soup with no bread. I mean—what kind of dinner is that?

CHILD 2: Yeah, who wants to have a dinner of nothing but warm soup? Yuck!

CHILD 3: I don't know about you two [points to Child 1 and Child 2], but this old lady sounds like she doesn't have a clue, if you know what I mean.

CHILD 1: Yeah, and then to top it all off she goes and whips all of her 24 children before she puts them in bed. I'll tell you one thing, this is one mean old lady.

CHILD 2: Yeah, I'm sure glad she's not my mother. Can you just imagine eating warm soup every night and then getting a beating just before bedtime? I think this old lady is just a little loony.

OLD WOMAN: Hey, who are you calling loony?

CHILD 2: Hey, listen lady, you're the one who's going around giving your kids some warm soup and beating them before bedtime.

CHILD 1: Yeah, and you're the one who puts all your 24 children into a stinky old shoe. What kid wants to live in a shoe? How about an apartment house?

OLD WOMAN: Hey, I can't help it if the stupid author person put me and my kids into a shoe. I'm just following orders.

CHILD 3: [sarcastically] Yeah, right! You're the grown-up here. Why can't you put your kids into a good house, give them some good food, and put them in some good beds for the night?

OLD WOMAN: Like I said, it's not my fault. It's that stupid author person. He made me do all that stuff. In fact, he's making us do all this stuff right now. I don't know about you guys but I've had it up to here [holds one hand parallel to the floor just under chin] with this author person.

CHILD 1: Yeah, so have I!

CHILD 2: Me, too!

CHILD 3: Yeah, me too!

NARRATOR: And so it was that the Old Woman finally moved out of the shoe and into a good neighborhood. She fed her children steaks and baked potatoes and salad and chocolate cream pie for dinner and she read them all wonderful bedtime stories and never beat any of them. And they all lived happily ever after. But all I can say to that stupid author person is that he better not show his face around here or he's going to be in big, big trouble.

OLD WOMAN: Yeah, REALLY BIG TROUBLE!!

CHILD 1: Yeah, what she said. [points to Old Woman]!

CHILD 2: Yeah, what she said. [points to Old Woman]!

CHILD 3: Yeah, what they said. [points to Child 1 and Child 2]!

The Hip-Hop Humpty Dumpty (by LL Cool Egg)

STAGING: There is no narrator for this script. The characters should all be standing around in a loose arrangement. Encourage the characters to sing (not read) their lines in typical hip-hop fashion. They may also want to get "in character"—walking and acting as some of their favorite musical artists might. You may wish to play a musical accompaniment in the background.

Singer 1	Singer 2	Singer 3
X	X	X

SINGER 1: We're gonna sing you this song
And it won't take long.
It's about a cool dude,
He's sometimes used for food.

SINGER 2: His name be Humpty Dumpty,
And not Rumpty Crumpty.
You've seen him in the morning and seen him in the night.
He's a Humpty Dumpty sight.

SINGER 3: Now is skin is jus' a shell,
And it makes him look real swell.
But it sometimes has a crack
From his head on down his back.

SINGER 1: Now some jus' eat him fried,
With some bacon on the side.
Or they boil him in a pan
With some hash from a can.

SINGER 2: He is real well known
In every time zone.
You can find him north and south.
You can find him in your mouth.

SINGER 3: You can find him in a box,
Behind the cream and lox.
He be hidin' on the shelf,
He be hidin' by himself,

SINGER 1: But mos' of the day
He be sittin' in a tray.
It don't bother me none
'Cause he be havin' fun.

SINGER 2: Now come a time ago,
This writer wanted dough.
He said, "This egg be needin' glory
This egg he needs a story."

SINGER 3: So he wrote an egg tale
And he made an egg sale,
'Bout a day upon a wall,
'Bout a day about a fall.

SINGER 1: See, this egg he wanted more,
Not the shelf inside the store.
He wanted to see far.

Yeah, he wanted a guitar.

SINGER 2: He wanted to be rockin,'
Kickin' back and really knockin.'
He really wanted out.
Of that we had no doubt.

SINGER 3: So one day he got a ladder.
He was feelin' fine, not madder.
He looked across the place
And a smile it crossed his face.

SINGER 1: What if I climb a wall?
What if I get real tall?
I could play a far out tune.
I could hip hop 'neath the moon.

SINGER 2: So, he climbed the ladder tall
Until he sat upon the wall.
And there he looked around.
And there he made a sound.

SINGER 3: A song began to form.
He started to perform.
He was dancin', he was groovin',
He was really up and movin'.

SINGER 1: He was swinging side to side.
He was on a magic ride.
The music started blaring.
All the cats they started staring.

SINGER 2: This Humpty Dumpty dude
Was really in the mood.
He boogied to and fro.
He was really in the flow.

SINGER 3: But his foot it took a slip,
And he took a sudden flip.
He done fall upon the ground,
And his parts went all around.

SINGER 1: [slowly] And the people they be sad,

SINGER 2: [slowly] For the rockin' egg they had.

SINGER 3: [slowly] Old Humpty he couldn't stop,

ALL: [slowly] Doin' the "Scrambled Egg Hip Hop."

Goldilocks and the Three Gorillas

STAGING: The narrators and the three gorillas may all be seated on tall stools or chairs. Each should have a music stand or lectern. Goldilocks, on the other hand, should hold a script in her hands and walk around the staging area.

		Papa Gorilla X	Mama Gorilla X	Baby Gorilla X	
	Goldilocks X				
Narrator 1 X					Narrator 2 X

NARRATOR 1: Once upon a time, in a far away place, there lived a family of gorillas. There was Papa Gorilla . . .

PAPA GORILLA: That's me!

NARRATOR: . . . Mama Gorilla . . .

MAMA GORILLA: That's me!

NARRATOR: . . . and Baby Gorilla.

BABY GORILLA: That's me!

NARRATOR 2: The three gorillas lived in a very large cottage in the middle of the woods. They were a happy gorilla family. They played together, they laughed together, and they went swinging in the forest together.

NARRATOR 1: Well, one day a little girl named Goldilocks . . .

GOLDILOCKS: That's me!

NARRATOR 1: . . . decided to go for a walk in the forest. She was curious as to what she might find there.

NARRATOR 2: At the same time, Mama Gorilla was working in her kitchen.

MAMA GORILLA: I'm making a fine cherry pie for us to eat. But in taking it out of the oven I see that it is very hot. It is far too hot to eat.

PAPA GORILLA: Well then, we should go in the forest and swing from the trees while the cherry pie is cooling.

BABY GORILLA: That sounds like fun. Let's go!

NARRATOR 2: And so the three gorillas left the cherry pie on the table to cool. They went into the forest to swing from the trees.

NARRATOR 1: Meanwhile, Goldilocks was coming down the path. As she turned the corner she saw the three gorillas' cottage. She walked up to the cottage and peered in the windows. As she looked inside she saw three plates of cherry pie on the table. She was very hungry and decided she wanted some cherry pie.

GOLDILOCKS: Yes, I am very hungry. I would like to have some cherry pie to eat.

NARRATOR 2: So Goldilocks opened the door of the cottage and walked inside. She touched Papa Gorilla's cherry pie.

GOLDILOCKS: Ohhhh, this is way too hot. It is much too hot for me to eat.

NARRATOR 1: Then she touched Mama Gorilla's cherry pie.

GOLDILOCKS: Ohhh, this is way too cool. It is much too cool for me to eat.

NARRATOR 2: Then she touched Baby Gorilla's cherry pie.

GOLDILOCKS: Ahhhh, this is just right!

NARRATOR 1: And with that, she ate up all of Baby Gorilla's cherry pie.

NARRATOR 2: Goldilocks then walked around the inside of the cottage. She saw the three chairs belonging to the three gorillas.

NARRATOR 1: First she sat down in Papa Gorilla's chair.

GOLDILOCKS: Ohhhh, this is much too big.

NARRATOR 2: Then she sat down in Mama Gorilla's chair.

GOLDILOCKS: Ohhhh, this is much too narrow.

NARRATOR 1: Then she sat down in Baby Gorilla's chair.

GOLDILOCKS: Ahhhh, this is just right.

NARRATOR 2: After a while Goldilocks decided to go upstairs and see what she could find. There she found the three gorillas' beds.

NARRATOR 1: First she lay down in Papa Gorilla's bed.

GOLDILOCKS: Ohhhh, this is much too soft.

NARRATOR 2: Then she lay down in Mama Gorilla's bed.

GOLDILOCKS: Ohhhh, this is much too hard.

NARRATOR 1: Then she lay down in Baby Gorilla's bed.

GOLDILOCKS: Ahhhh, this is just right.

NARRATOR 2: And she fell fast asleep.

NARRATOR 1: Before long the three gorillas came back from the forest. As soon as they walked in the door, they could see that something was wrong.

PAPA GORILLA: Who's been eating my cherry pie?

MAMA GORILLA: Who's been eating my cherry pie?

BABY GORILLA: Who's been eating my cherry pie? And it's all gone!

NARRATOR 2: The three gorillas went into the living room. As soon as they walked in, they could see that something was wrong.

PAPA GORILLA: Who's been sitting in my chair?

MAMA GORILLA: Who's been sitting in my chair?

BABY GORILLA: Who's been sitting in my chair? And it's all broken!

NARRATOR 1: Then the three gorillas went upstairs. As soon as they walked into the bedroom, they could see that something was wrong.

PAPA GORILLA: Who's been sleeping in my bed?

MAMA GORILLA: Who's been sleeping in my bed?

BABY GORILLA: Who's been sleeping in my bed? And she's right there!

NARRATOR 2: With that, Goldilocks woke up. When she saw the three gorillas standing over her she got so frightened that she ran as fast as she could from the house.

PAPA GORILLA: Who's running away from our house?

MAMA GORILLA: Who's running away from our house?

BABY GORILLA: Who's running away from our house?

GOLDILOCKS: I'm running away from your house, you big gorillas. And I'm never coming back!

A Very Strange Tale About a Very Strange Boy

STAGING: Narrator 1 may be seated on a tall stool to the left of the staging area; Narrator 2 may be seated on a tall stool to the right. The other characters should be standing and walking around the staging area.

```
Narrator 1                                                Narrator 2
   X                                                          X
                  Villager 1      Villager 2    Villager 3
                      X               X             X
         Boy
          X
```

NARRATOR 1: Once upon a time in a small village in a small country, there lived a shepherd boy.

NARRATOR 2: Now, we should point out that a shepherd boy is a boy who takes care of shepherds.

NARRATOR 1: No, he's not, silly. A shepherd boy is a young boy who was given the job of watching over a herd of sheep.

NARRATOR 2: I've heard of sheep!

NARRATOR 1: Not that kind of "heard." A herd of sheep is a whole bunch of sheep all in one place.

NARRATOR 2: Oh, I get it! [puzzled] I think.

NARRATOR 1: Anyway, as I was saying, . . . there was this shepherd boy in a small village in a small country a long time ago.

NARRATOR 2: Hey, maybe I might want to be a shepherd some day. You know, after we do all this narrator stuff we might want to take a look at another job. Like maybe a job as a shepherd. Anyway, how much money does a shepherd make?

NARRATOR 1: [getting frustrated] I don't know and I don't care! Besides, it has nothing to do with the story we're trying to tell.

NARRATOR 2: [surprised] Oh, OK. Then go ahead.

NARRATOR 1: Anyway, as I was saying [stares at Narrator 2], . . . there was this shepherd boy and he was asked to take care of the village flock. That is, his job was to take care of all the sheep that belonged to the village.

NARRATOR 2: Hey, what's a flock? Can I buy one at the store? Can I get one at McDonald's? Will I find one in my box of cereal?

NARRATOR 1: No, you can't, and no, you won't! A flock is like a group or a whole bunch of something.

NARRATOR 2: Oh, like a whole flock of kids on the playground?

NARRATOR 1: No, you can't have a flock of students. You can only have a flock of animals, like sheep.

NARRATOR 2: [surprised] Oh, I get it!

NARRATOR 1: [mad] I hope you do!

NARRATOR 2: So, there he was one day just sitting around watching these stupid sheep. . . .

NARRATOR 1: Hey, look, sheep aren't stupid, they just don't do very much except chew grass and mess up the lawn.

NARRATOR 2: OK.

NARRATOR 1: Can I continue?

NARRATOR 2: Yeah, I said OK!

NARRATOR 1: [somewhat frustrated] Anyway, so, the little boy was sitting around—bored out of his skull—when he got a great idea. "I'll fool the villagers," he said, "because I'm really very bored and need something to amuse myself."

NARRATOR 2: So what did he do?

NARRATOR 1: He yelled!

BOY: [loudly] Reptiles! Reptiles! Help! Help! Reptiles are chasing the sheep!!

NARRATOR 2: All the villagers heard the cries of the little shepherd boy and ran up the hill to help drive the reptiles away.

VILLAGER 1: Hey, little shepherd boy, didn't you just yell "Reptiles?"

BOY: Yes, I did.

VILLAGER 2: [frustrated] Well, we just ran all the way up this hill only to find that there are no reptiles anywhere to be found. There are no snakes. There are no crocodiles, or lizards, or turtles to be found anywhere.

VILLAGER 3: Yeah, the sheep are all quietly munching on their grass, and there are no reptiles anywhere. Were you kidding us?

BOY: Why, yes I was. It just gets so boring around here watching these stupid sheep . . . .

NARRATOR 1: Now, wait a minute. Like I said before, sheep aren't stupid. So maybe they can't do two-column subtraction, but that doesn't mean they're dumb.

BOY: Anyway, it's really boring here.

NARRATOR 2: Well, all the villagers were really ticked off at the little shepherd boy for fooling them like that. And they all went back down the hill to the village, where they were all watching the latest episode of *American Idol*.

NARRATOR 1: Hey, wait a minute. This story takes place a long time ago. . . a long time ago before televisions were even invented.

NARRATOR 2: Oh, OK. Maybe they just went back to the village and sat around watching grass grow.

NARRATOR 1: Well, anyway, the boy was still back on the hill watching his sheep. And getting even more bored. So he decided to have some more fun and he yelled. . . .

BOY: Reptiles! Reptiles!! The reptiles are coming to get the sheep!!!

NARRATOR 2: I bet I know what happened.

NARRATOR 1: That's right. All the villagers ran up the hill to see what all the commotion was about.

NARRATOR 2: Yeah, 'cause they didn't want those big old hairy reptiles messing around with their cute little sheep.

NARRATOR 1: Hey, reptiles aren't hairy. My father is hairy, but reptiles aren't hairy!

NARRATOR 2: [amazed] Oh. OK.

NARRATOR 1: So the villagers ran up the hill. But when they got to the top they just saw the little shepherd boy laughing away.

BOY: Ha, ha, ha. Ha, ha, ha.

VILLAGER 1: [angry] Hey, little shepherd boy. Did you fool us again by yelling "Reptiles" when there were no reptiles at all?

BOY: Yes, I did.

VILLAGER 2: [angry] You know, that isn't very nice.

BOY: Yes, but it's so gosh darn boring up here with these sheep, I just wanted something to do.

VILLAGER 3: [very angry] Well, perhaps you can find a video game or something. We're getting sick and tired of your stupid pranks. We can't keep running up here every time you yell something.

VILLAGER 1: You should save your yelling for when there is something really wrong.

VILLAGER 2: Don't cry "Reptiles!" when there are no reptiles!

VILLAGER 3: [pointing to Villager 2] Yeah, what he said.

NARRATOR 1: With that, all the villagers climbed back down the hill once again. They were all pretty ticked at the little shepherd boy.

NARRATOR 2: I bet I can guess what happened next.

NARRATOR 1: You're probably right. The little shepherd boy saw a real reptile prowling about his flock of sheep. Alarmed, he leaped to his feet and yelled as loudly as he could . . .

BOY: REPTILE! REPTILE!!

NARRATOR 2: I bet the villagers thought that he was trying to fool them again.

NARRATOR 1: You're right. They thought he was fooling them again. So they didn't do anything. They waited . . . and waited . . . and waited. But at sunset, everybody wondered why the little shepherd boy hadn't returned to the village with all the sheep.

VILLAGER 1: Where's that little shepherd boy?

VILLAGER 2: Where's our sheep?

VILLAGER 3: Let's go see.

NARRATOR 2: So what did they discover?

NARRATOR 1: The villagers went up the hill. There was the little shepherd boy, but all the sheep were gone.

BOY: There really was a big hairy reptile here. He came and ate all the sheep. Now, all the sheep are gone. I yelled "Reptile." Why didn't you come?

VILLAGER 1: We thought you were fooling us again.

VILLAGERS 2 & 3: [pointing to Villager 1] Yeah, what he said.

NARRATOR 1: So it was that the village lost all its sheep to the big hairy reptile.

NARRATOR 2: But what happened to the boy?

NARRATOR 1: Well, he got bored again. And so one day, while he was watching the flock of sheep, he yelled something.

NARRATOR 2: What did he yell?

NARRATOR 1: Mammals, mammals, MAMMALS!!

Some Story Characters Get Really, Really Mad (And I Mean TOTALLY Mad!)

STAGING: The narrator may be placed on a tall stool or be standing to one side of the staging area. The characters should be walking around throughout the presentation. (Please note that the audience has a part in this script.)

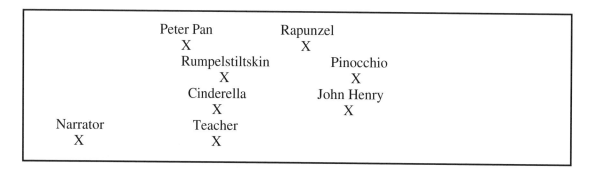

	Peter Pan X	Rapunzel X
	Rumpelstiltskin X	Pinocchio X
	Cinderella X	John Henry X
Narrator X	Teacher X	

NARRATOR: Once upon a . . .

PETER PAN: [interrupting] Hey, hold it just a minute.

NARRATOR: What seems to be the problem?

PETER PAN: [irritated] Look, I've been looking at all the stories in this readers theatre book. There are stories about some wolves and a pig, there are stories about Little Red Riding Hood, there are stories about Mary and her little lamb, and there are stories about some egg guy who falls off a wall. But you know what? There's not even one little story about me. Not one! I used to be a pretty popular guy in the story business. How come that author person didn't include any scripts about me in his collection?

NARRATOR: Hey, I'm just a character here. I do what the author tells me to do.

RAPUNZEL: You know, Peter's right. I'm a pretty important character as far as fairy tales go. I've got this great-looking hair, which I let grow long. And then I let my hair down and this really good-looking guy climbs up my hair. And then we fall in love and get married and all that stuff. So how come the author guy didn't write a readers theatre script about me?

NARRATOR: [soothing] Hey, keep your shirts on. Maybe he didn't have enough room in the book to include all you guys.

RUMPELSTILTSKIN: Hey, he had enough room to include that weird little chicken guy who runs around yelling his head off [see part 4]. And he had enough room to put in that Goldilocks character who always seems to wriggle her way into every story. And he sure had enough room to include that Peter, Peter, Pumpkin-eater guy in here. So how come he doesn't have enough room for the rest of us?

NARRATOR: Whoa, slow down guys.

PINOCCHIO: [mad] Yeah, Rumpy's right! You know, come to think of it, the writer never included me in any story—not in this book, not in his last book, not in any book in between. Boy, that really stinks! You know, after all the pleasure I've given kids all these years, the least that writer could do was to create one teeny, tiny script with me in it. But, nooooooooo! Apparently, he had much better things to do.

NARRATOR: Hey, hold on, guys! This is getting out of hand. You guys have just got to settle down. There must be some logical explanation here somewhere.

CINDERELLA: [angry] Explanation, Shmecksplanation! I can't believe what I'm seeing. Who does that writer think he is? Aren't I one of the loveliest and most beautiful and most gorgeous story characters who ever appeared in a book? I mean, kids have been reading about me for years. But do you think that writer has one brain cell large enough to think about including me in his book? [shakes her fist] Oh, boy, just wait till I get my hands on him.

JOHN HENRY: [frustrated] Hey, this writer guy just doesn't have a clue . . . not a clue! After all, aren't I one of the strongest characters in any American folktale? And where does he put me? NOWHERE, that's where. Not a single word! Not a single page! Not a single story! Nothing! It's obvious this writer person doesn't know much about anything.

NARRATOR: Hey, guys, let's settle down.

PETER PAN: [really angry] Settle down, are you kidding? This writer person, whoever he may be, has just slighted some of the most beautiful, most important, and most memorable story characters in all of literature.

RAPUNZEL: [really mad] Yeah, who does he think he is? Here we are, waiting around for some decent story so we can do our parts, and he goes off writing tales about guys that look like an egg and a bunch of mice running around on a clock and an old lady who lives in a big fat smelly shoe and all that other stuff. It's just not fair! It's just not fair!

RUMPELSTILTSKIN: [loud] Boy, you got that right!

NARRATOR: Whoa, this is getting way out of hand.

86

PINOCCHIO: [very mad] Hey, step aside, narrator person. We're taking over now. I think we've all about had it up to here with that writer guy and his weird ideas. He's probably in it just for the money. Yeah, that's it. He thinks he can just write a couple of readers theatre scripts with some minor characters, print them up in some book called *MORE Tadpole Tales and Other Totally Terrific Treats for Readers Theatre*, sell those books to teachers and librarians all over the country, and then retire to some beach in Hawaii with his lovely wife and a fancy-dancy car. And what happens to us? Nothing! That's what! Nada!

CINDERELLA: [fuming] Oh, just wait till I get my hands on him. I'm so angry I could take my glass slipper and throw it right at his pointy little head.

NARRATOR: You guys are getting way too upset over all this. I'm sure there's some good reason why the author guy didn't include all of you in his book. But that's no reason why you all have to fly off the handle and get all upset and all that stuff.

JOHN HENRY: [angry] Hey, I know. Why don't we just all get together and go to is house and tell him a thing or two? What do you say, guys? Are you ready?

ALL: Yes, YES, **YES**! [They all storm offstage.]

NARRATOR: [directly to the audience] Well, there you have it. Just as I was trying to tell you guys a really nice story all the characters just up and left me. [thinks for awhile] Hey, wait a minute, I have an idea. Why don't you [points to audience] write your own scripts with some of the characters who didn't get into this book? [points to copy of the book]

AUDIENCE: Cool!

NARRATOR: [excited] You know, the more I think about it, the more I like that idea. So, here's what you should do. Tell your nice teacher person [points to teacher] that you want some time to write your own readers theatre scripts just like the author of this book did. [There are some really cool ideas on how to do that in chapter 1.] You can use some of the characters the author left out of the book or invent some of your own. Put those characters into some really funny scripts or make them do some really funny things. Then ask your really cool teacher [points to teacher] how you can print up your scripts. Then you can present one or more of those readers theatre scripts in the classroom or to other classes in the school. And then you'll be really famous . . . really, really famous. And you'll make lots and lots of money, and you'll be able to retire from school and move to a beach in Hawaii and have a fancy-dancy car . . . just like the author of *MORE Tadpole Tales and Other Totally Terrific Treats for Readers Theatre* did. And you'll all live happily ever after!

AUDIENCE: Wow, cool!

TEACHER: I think it's a terrific idea! What do you say, guys? Shall we do it?

AUDIENCE: Yes, YES, **YES**!

PART III

Here's Some Tadpole Tales
(Just Like It Says on the Cover of the Book)

The Little Green Tadpole

STAGING: The characters should all be placed behind music stands or lecterns. The narrator may stand off to the side and away from the other characters. As appropriate, you may wish to explain to students what algae is before this script is presented.

	Fish	Water Bug	Frog	
	X	X	X	
Little Green Tadpole				
X				
				Narrator
				X

NARRATOR: Once upon a time there was a little green tadpole. She lived in a pond with a fish, a water bug, and a frog. One day the Little Green Tadpole found some algae [al-GEE] on the bottom of the pond.

LITTLE GREEN TADPOLE: Who will help me get the algae [al-GEE]?

FISH: Not I!

WATER BUG: Not I!

FROG: Not I!

From *MORE Tadpole Tales and Other Totally Terrific Treats for Readers Theatre* by Anthony D. Fredericks. Santa Barbara, CA: Libraries Unlimited. Copyright © 2010.

LITTLE GREEN TADPOLE:	OK, then I will get it myself.
NARRATOR:	And she did! The Little Green Tadpole got the algae [al-GEE]. She got some algae [al-GEE] here. And she got some algae [al-GEE] there. Finally she had lots and lots of algae [al-GEE].
LITTLE GREEN TADPOLE:	Who will help me cut up the algae?
FISH:	Not I!
WATER BUG:	Not I!
FROG:	Not I!
LITTLE GREEN TADPOLE:	OK, then I will cut it myself.
NARRATOR:	And she did! The Little Green Tadpole cut and cut the algae. She cut all the algae and put it into a large pile. There was a lot of algae in the pile. The algae was ready to be put into smaller piles.
LITTLE GREEN TADPOLE:	Who will help me put the algae into smaller piles?
FISH:	Not I!
WATER BUG:	Not I!
FROG:	Not I!
LITTLE GREEN TADPOLE:	OK, then I will do it myself.
NARRATOR:	And she did! The Little Green Tadpole made small piles. She made one small pile. And, she made another small pile. And she made another small pile. She made lots and lots of small piles. The piles were ready to be taken to her house.
LITTLE GREEN TADPOLE:	Who will help me take the algae to my house?
FISH:	Not I!

WATER BUG: Not I!

FROG: Not I!

LITTLE GREEN TADPOLE: OK, then I will take it myself.

NARRATOR: And she did! The Little Green Tadpole took the first pile to her house. She took the second pile to her house. She took the third pile to her house. When she was done there were many piles in her house.

LITTLE GREEN TADPOLE: Who will help me store these piles?

FISH: Not I!

WATER BUG: Not I!

FROG: Not I!

LITTLE GREEN TADPOLE: OK, then I will store them myself.

NARRATOR: And she did! The Little Green Tadpole stored each pile in her kitchen. Pile after pile went into her kitchen. Pretty soon her kitchen was filled with piles of algae. Her kitchen smelled very good . . . very, very good!

The fish, the water bug, and the frog smelled the piles of algae. They dashed to her house to get some. The Little Green Tadpole put the algae on the table.

LITTLE GREEN TADPOLE: Who will help me eat the good algae?

FISH: I will!

WATER BUG: I will!

FROG: I will!

LITTLE GREEN
TADPOLE: Oh, no, you won't! You guys don't eat algae. You guys don't even like algae. You guys eat other stuff . . . not algae. So get out of here and leave me alone! Good-bye!

NARRATOR: And she ate up all the algae herself.

LITTLE GREEN
TADPOLE: Yum, yum, yum!

One Day in the Swamp

STAGING: The narrator stands off to the side of the staging area or may sit on a tall stool. The other characters form a loose semicircle or may walk around as they are speaking.

```
        Narrator
        X
                            Tadpole        Frog
                            X              X
              Starter
              X
```

NARRATOR: Once upon a time there lived a tadpole and a frog. The frog, because he was older, thought he was a fast swimmer. The tadpole, because he had a long tail, thought he was a fast swimmer.

FROG: Hey, tadpole, I'm the fastest thing in the swamp. There is nobody who can beat me.

TADPOLE: I may be small, but I'm much faster than you.

FROG: Oh, yeah? Who says?

TADPOLE: I say so.

FROG: Well, if you think you're so fast, then why don't we race?

TADPOLE: OK, you're on!

NARRATOR: The frog and the tadpole agreed to the race. They would race through the swamp, up and around an old log, and back through the weeds near the shore. It would be the race of the year!

FROG: Yeah, I'm going to beat the pants off that little tadpole.

TADPOLE: Hey, wise guy, in case you didn't notice, tadpoles don't wear pants.

FROG: Well, I'm going to beat you just the same.

TADPOLE: Yeah, we'll see about that!

NARRATOR: All the other animals lined up around the swamp to watch the big race.

STARTER: It is now time for the race. The winner will be the first one to cross the finish line. Frog, are you ready?

FROG: Yes.

STARTER: Tadpole, are you ready?

TADPOLE: Yes.

STARTER: Then, on your marks. Get set. GO!

NARRATOR: Both the tadpole and the frog zoomed across the start line. The frog was doing his best frog kick. The tadpole was flicking his tail back and forth as fast as he could. Because the tadpole lived in the water more than the frog, he was speeding ahead of the frog.

FROG: Oh, no. That little runt is going faster than me. And soon he will beat me.

NARRATOR: The tadpole got further and further ahead of the frog. He made the turn at the old log and was headed back toward the finish line. In a few minutes he would cross the finish line. Then he made a terrible mistake.

TADPOLE: I think I'll just stick my head out of the water to see where that silly old frog is.

NARRATOR: The tadpole stuck his head out of the water. But right there in front of him was a big blue heron. A big, blue, and very hungry heron. And quick as a wink, that tadpole became part of the heron's dinner.

AUDIENCE: OHHHHHHH, NOOOOOOOO!

FROG: Hey, what's all that noise about? I think I'll go see.

NARRATOR: And that's when the frog made the same terrible mistake that the tadpole had. And he too became someone's dinner. Of course nobody won the race. But that wouldn't be much of a story.

STARTER: No, that wouldn't be much of a story.

NARRATOR: So a bunch of writers got together. They decided they didn't like frogs or tadpoles.

STARTER: They were sort of weird!

NARRATOR: Yeah, all writers are weird. But anyway, these writers decided to change things a bit. They decided to make up a story about a rabbit and a turtle who raced each other.

STARTER: Where the heck did they find a rabbit and a turtle?

NARRATOR: Who knows? Writers like to do strange things like that. So anyway, they made up a story about a rabbit and a turtle. And in their story nobody ate the two contestants.

STARTER: That's too bad; I hear rabbit stew and turtle soup are pretty good!

The Three Tadpoles and the Big Ugly Fish

STAGING: The characters may all be standing behind music stands. Or to add a little movement, you may have the three tadpoles "swim" under an imaginary "bridge" (under a long table in the middle of the staging area).

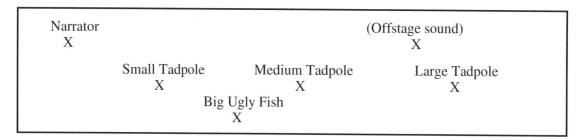

Narrator				(Offstage sound)
X				X
	Small Tadpole	Medium Tadpole		Large Tadpole
	X	X		X
		Big Ugly Fish		
		X		

NARRATOR: Once upon a time there were three tadpoles who lived in a pond down in the valley. One day they decided to travel to a new pond up the stream. On their way to the new pond they had to swim under a large bridge. And underneath the bridge there lived an ugly, one-eyed, and very big fish. Before anyone could swim under the bridge, they had to get permission from the ugly, one-eyed, and ugly fish.

He never gave permission—he just ate anyone who happened to come along.

Well, one day the three tadpoles decided they weren't afraid of the big ugly fish. Besides, the new pond had lots of good things to eat. So they swam up the stream and came to the bridge. The small tadpole was the first one to reach the bridge. He began to swim under it.

(OFFSTAGE SOUND): Swim, swim. Swim, swim. Swim, swim.

BIG UGLY FISH: [growling] Who's that swimming under my bridge?

SMALL TADPOLE: [in a squeaky voice] It's only me. I'm going up the stream to the new pond.

BIG UGLY FISH: [angry] Oh, no, you're not! I'm going to eat you for breakfast!

SMALL TADPOLE: [pleading] Oh, please don't, Mr. Big Ugly One-Eyed Fish. I'm only the smallest tadpole. I'm much too tiny for you to eat. And besides, I wouldn't taste very good. Why don't you wait for my brother, the second tadpole? He's much bigger than me and he would be much tastier.

NARRATOR: The big ugly fish thought about that for a while and decided that he didn't want to waste his time on such a little tadpole—especially if there was a bigger tadpole coming along.

BIG UGLY FISH: All right. You can swim under my bridge. Go and eat all the good stuff in the new pond. Besides, you'll be fatter and I can eat you when you return.

NARRATOR: So the smallest tadpole swam under the bridge and up to the new pond.

The big ugly fish did not have to wait long for the second tadpole.

(OFFSTAGE SOUND): Swim, swim. Swim, swim. Swim, swim.

BIG UGLY FISH: [growling] Who's that swimming under my bridge?

MEDIUM TADPOLE: It's just me. I'm going up to the new pond to get some good stuff to eat.

BIG UGLY FISH: [angry] Oh, no, you're not. I'm going to eat you for breakfast.

MEDIUM TADPOLE: [pleading] Oh, please don't. I may be bigger than the first tadpole, but I'm much smaller than my brother, the third tadpole. Why don't you wait for him? He would be a much better meal than me.

NARRATOR: The big ugly fish was getting hungrier . . . very, very hungry. But he did not want to waste his appetite on a middle-sized tadpole—especially if there was a much larger tadpole coming along.

BIG UGLY FISH: [gruff] All right. You can swim under my bridge. Go get nice and fat in the new pond and I'll eat you on your way back.

NARRATOR: So the medium tadpole swam under the bridge and up to the new pond. Very soon thereafter, the third tadpole began to swim under the bridge.

(OFFSTAGE SOUND): Swim, swim. Swim, swim. Swim, swim.

BIG UGLY FISH: [growling] Who's that swimming under my bridge?

LARGE TADPOLE: [in a deep voice] It's just me. I'm going up to the new pond to eat some good stuff.

BIG UGLY FISH: [angry] Oh, no, you're not! I'm going to eat you for breakfast!

LARGE TADPOLE: That's what you think!

NARRATOR: The large tadpole suddenly turned into a frog—a big frog. A big, giant, enormous frog. A big, giant, enormous, and very hungry frog. A VERY hungry frog. A VERY hungry frog who loved to eat fish. A VERY hungry frog who loved to eat big, ugly one-eyed fish. A VERY hungry frog who loved to eat big, ugly one-eyed fish that lived under a certain bridge.

100

FROG (AKA LARGE TADPOLE): Now it's time for breakfast.

(OFFSTAGE SOUND): Chomp, chomp. Chomp, chomp. Chomp, chomp.

NARRATOR: The frog (also known as the Large Tadpole) swam under the bridge and joined his two brothers, or tadpoles, in the new pond. They spent the rest of the day enjoying all the good stuff to eat in their new home. The next morning the two remaining tadpoles turned into frogs. And they all lived happily ever after.

Mama and Papa Tadpole

STAGING: The narrator may stand behind a podium or lectern. All the other characters may be seated in chairs.

Mama Tadpole	Papa Tadpole	Baby Frog
X	X	X
(Offstage Voice)		
X		
	Narrator	
	X	

NARRATOR: Once upon a time there was Papa Tadpole . . .

PAPA TADPOLE: Hi.

NARRATOR: There was Mama Tadpole . . .

MAMA TADPOLE: Hi.

NARRATOR: They both lived in a pond. They were very happy. Papa Tadpole worked in an office. Mama Tadpole was a teacher. Sometimes they would all sit in the yard. They were very happy.

PAPA TADPOLE:	Hey, how can we talk? We're just tadpoles. We don't even have lips!
NARRATOR:	The writer person made you talk. You can talk like a boy. You can talk like a girl. You can talk like a grown-up.
PAPA TADPOLE:	You're right! We can talk like people.
MAMA TADPOLE:	But what if we don't want to talk? What if we just want to burp?
NARRATOR:	It's not up to me. But some author wrote this story. He wanted you to talk. He wanted you to say something. Something important. Something important about a frog.
MAMA TADPOLE:	Wait a minute!. Why a frog? Frogs are ugly! Frogs are slimy! Frogs are no fun! How did a frog get into this story?
NARRATOR:	I don't know. It was the writer's idea. He wrote the story. Maybe he knows.
PAPA TADPOLE:	You know, the Narrator has a point. Maybe we should listen to the story. Let's hear what happens.
MAMA TADPOLE:	OK.
NARRATOR:	OK, you two ready now?
PAPA & MAMA TADPOLE:	[together] Yes!
NARRATOR:	OK. One day Mama was cleaning the house. Papa was working in the garage. Suddenly a baby frog hopped into the story.
PAPA TADPOLE:	How did the baby frog get in the story?
MAMA TADPOLE:	Yeah, how did the baby frog get in this story?
NARRATOR:	I don't know. The writer just put him there.
PAPA TADPOLE:	OK.
MAMA TADPOLE:	OK.

NARRATOR:	So, this baby frog hopped into the story. And it was an ugly baby frog.
BABY FROG:	Hey, careful. Baby frogs have feelings, too.
NARRATOR:	Sorry about that.
MAMA TADPOLE:	OK, so now there's a baby frog in our story.
PAPA TADPOLE:	So, we said, "Hey, how did that baby frog get here?"
NARRATOR:	Sad to say, nobody knew the answer.
PAPA TADPOLE:	What do you think, Mr. Narrator?
NARRATOR:	I'm not allowed to think. So, I don't know.
MAMA TADPOLE:	Well, I hope I don't grow up to be an ugly baby frog.
PAPA TADPOLE:	Yes, I hope I don't grow up to be an ugly baby frog.
MAMA TADPOLE:	Yes, that would be terrible.
PAPA TADPOLE:	It would be very terrible.
BABY FROG:	It's not so terrible.
MAMA TADPOLE:	Why do you say that?
BABY FROG:	Well, I can hop. I can croak. And I have lots of slime on my body.
PAPA TADPOLE:	Oh, that's gross!
MAMA TADPOLE:	Yeah, that's gross!
BABY FROG:	It's not so bad. I get to eat flies all day.
PAPA TADPOLE:	Oh, that's gross!
MAMA TADPOLE:	Yeah, that's gross!
BABY FROG:	Not really. I get to sleep on lily pads.
PAPA TADPOLE:	I wouldn't like that!
MAMA TADPOLE:	Me either!
BABY FROG:	And I spend all day going "Ribbit, ribbit, ribbit!"

PAPA TADPOLE: I don't have lips. I couldn't do that.

MAMA TADPOLE: Me either!

NARRATOR: [interrupting] Hey, it's almost the end of the story.

MAMA TADPOLE: Well, OK.

PAPA TADPOLE: I don't like what frogs do.

MAMA TADPOLE: Me either!

PAPA TADPOLE: It wouldn't be fun being a frog.

MAMA TADPOLE: I think you're right.

PAPA TADPOLE: I hope we never become frogs.

MAMA TADPOLE: Yeah, that would be terrible!

NARRATOR: And so they both stayed home. Then one day something strange happened. Something weird happened. They suddenly turned into . . . into . . .

(OFFSTAGE VOICE): FROGS!

NARRATOR: And they both lived happily ever after.

A Tale of Two Tadpoles

STAGING: The narrator may stand to the side or behind the two major characters. The two tadpoles stand in front of the staging area.

Narrator X		
	Billy Tadpole X	Bobbie Tadpole X

NARRATOR: Once upon a time there were these two tadpoles. Now, they just weren't your average tadpoles. No sir. These two were the best looking and most intelligent tadpoles in the entire swamp. Not only were they good looking and smart, they were stars on the all-pond football team, they were two of the fastest sprinters on the school track team, and they found time to volunteer at the "Old Frogs Home" on the weekend. As you might imagine they were very, very popular—so much so that all the girl tadpoles in town wanted to go out on a date with these two handsome dudes. Anyway, these two sure did get a lot of attention.

BILLY: Hi, Bobbie, what's happenin'?

BOBBIE: Not much, dude. What's new in your neck of the pond?

BILLY: Oh, you know, same old, same old! Hey, I was just going to paddle on over to McTadpole's and get something good to eat. You want to come along?

BOBBIE: Sounds cool. Let's go.

NARRATOR: The two tadpoles wiggle over to McTadpole's and place their order. Billy orders a double bugburger with extra algae, some flies, and a chocolate shake. Bobbie orders two fish sandwiches, an extra large order of flies, and a Burp-a-Cola. When their order comes they swim on over to a table and begin eating.

BILLY: I don't know about you, Bobbie, but I'm getting a little tired of having all those girls stare at me in math class. It's really starting to get on my nerves. I can't do anything or go anywhere without those stupid girls following me around.

BOBBIE: Yeah, I know how you feel. They just keep staring at us, or sending us notes in social studies, or even hanging out around our lockers. Like you said, we can't go anywhere or do anything without those silly girls always in our face. And now they're trying to whistle at us with those funny looking lips of theirs.

BILLY: I sure wish they would find something better to do with their time than follow us around all the time. It's really starting to bug me. Get it? Bug me!

BOBBIE: Yeah, I got it all right! And I'm getting just as tired of it as you are. I know we're good looking, and smart, and athletic, and all that, but come on girls, give us a break!

BILLY: Well, you do know, Bobbie, that when we get older we're really going to get ugly. We're going to turn into really ugly frogs. We'll have warts all over our skin, our eyes will be bugging out, our skin will be slimy and slippery, we'll have big long tongues, and we'll have those big old ugly flippers at the ends of our feet. And then nobody will want to look at us or even go out on a date with us.

BOBBIE: You know, you're right, Billy. We will really be two ugly frogs. No one will even want to give us the time of day. We'll be spending most of our time capturing flies, or hopping around lily pads, or covering our bodies with lots and lots of slime.

BILLY: Yeah, it sure doesn't look like we've got a bright future ahead of us.

BOBBIE: Yeah, but you know what scares me the most?

BILLY: What's that?

BOBBIE: I'm really scared about those princesses who live in the nearby castle. Before too long they'll want to come down to the pond and plant their big fat lips on us to see if they can turn us into handsome princes.

BILLY: Boy, that is scary!

BOBBIE: You bet it is! So what do you say about getting out of here while the getting is good?

BILLY: You're on! Let's go!

NARRATOR: And so the two good-looking and very smart tadpoles swam off into the sunset. And they were never heard from again. [in an aside to the audience] Personally, I think they disguised themselves as alligators and are now living somewhere in Florida.

PART IV

This Is the Part That Always Comes after Part III (and before Part V)—Yeah, the Part That Has Some Unfinished Scripts and Partial Stories for Your Students to Complete (Pretty Neat, Huh?)

Wow, are we having fun or what? I'm sure that your students are just bubbling over with excitement and brimming with unmitigated joy—not to mention all the hilarity and laughter that comes from a language arts program that incorporates readers theatre into its design. Not only are your students excited about all the cool things their (totally cool) teacher has been doing with readers theatre; their parents are sending you all sorts of wonderful notes about how the students are absolutely captivated by readers theatre. ("You are simply the best teacher ever, and my wife and I would like to recommend you for the Nobel Prize.") You've undoubtedly received the praise and admiration of your building principal ("I have been blown away by your teaching excellence and would like to offer you a three-week vacation in Hawaii—all expenses paid!") and have been alerted to some sort of high honor or incredible recognition by the school board ("Go ahead—name your own salary for next year!") or some other community group in town ("I certainly think that the least we can do is get him a BMW to replace that 12-year-old wreck he drives to school every day!"). People all over town are singing your praises and erecting statues in your honor and naming streets after you and having parades celebrating your accomplishments and . . . and . . . but I digress!

Let's just say that something magical has happened in your classroom! And now you can increase that "Magic Quotient" one more time with the following stories. You see, the stories in this section of the book are designed to serve as starters for your students' own self-created readers theatre scripts. In each case a story has been set up, but not finished. Students should be encouraged to select a "story starter" and complete it using their own ideas and conclusions. Students can add to these scripts, modify them, or alter them in accordance with their own interests, logic, or warped senses of humor (pretty neat idea, huh?). You may find it appropriate for students to work on these scripts in small groups, rather than on an individual basis. Of course, there is no right or wrong way to complete any single story; instead, students may invent their own plots or themes as they see fit. Be sure to provide sufficient opportunities for student groups to share their stories with other members of the class or with another class in your school. You may also wish to consider filming these "productions" (or posting them on YouTube); who knows, there may be a future Hollywood legend in your class! ("I accept this Oscar and wish to thank the Academy and especially Mrs. Jones, my wonderful second grade teacher, who gave me my first start in film and continues to be my lifelong inspiration.")

All Cracked Up!

STAGING: The characters may be seated on stools or chairs. They may also be standing or positioned at individual lecterns.

```
                                    Boy 1
                        Girl 2       X          Boy 2
            Girl 1       X                       X        Big Bad Wolf
            X                                              X
Humpty Dumpty
    X
```

GIRL 1: Hello, audience. [waves to the audience]

GIRL 2: Yes, hello, audience. [waves to audience]

BOY 1: We are happy to be here!

BOY 2: Yes, we have a funny story to share.

BIG BAD WOLF: Grumble, grumble, grumble

GIRL 1: Hey, why is the Big Bad Wolf in this story?

GIRL 2: I don't know. Do you know? [points to Boy 1]

BOY 1: I don't know. Do you know? [points to Boy 2]

BOY 2: I don't know why he is here. He sure looks strange.

BIG BAD WOLF:	Yeah, why am I here? I think the author made a big mistake.
GIRL 1:	What do you mean?
BIG BAD WOLF:	I don't think the writer of this story is very smart.
GIRL 2:	Yeah, you're right. Isn't this a story about a big egg?
BOY 1:	Yes, it is. It's a story about a big egg, not a big bad wolf.
BOY 2:	Yeah, I don't think the writer was paying attention.
BIG BAD WOLF:	So is it OK if I leave?

POSSIBLE CONCLUSIONS

1. The Big Bad Wolf catches Humpty Dumpty when he falls off the wall and becomes a hero in the town.

2. The Big Bad Wolf and Humpty Dumpty decide to visit Little Red Riding Hood at her grandmother's house.

3. The Big Bad Wolf and Humpty Dumpty decide to go to the diner for breakfast. Everything changes, however, when the waitress serves scrambled eggs.

4. The Big Bad Wolf leaves this story for another story on the other side of town. Humpty Dumpty falls off the wall and doesn't live happily ever after.

5. Your idea.

The Mouse and the Clock

STAGING: There is no narrator for this script. The "mouse" should be standing and may move around the staging area. The other characters may be seated on chairs or stools.

Mouse X	Person 1 X	Person 2 X	Person 3 X

MOUSE: Hi, I'm a mouse

PERSON 1: You look cute.

MOUSE: Why, thank you.

PERSON 2: You look fast.

MOUSE: Yes, I am. I can run real fast.

PERSON 3: And, you look smart.

MOUSE: I'm smarter than my teacher!

PERSON 1: So, let's tell a story about you.

MOUSE: I'd like that!

PERSON 2: Yes, we'll tell a story.

MOUSE: Will I be the hero?

PERSON 3: Of course!

MOUSE: Good!

PERSON 1: It's a story called "Hickory, . . .

PERSON 2: "Dickory, . . .

PERSON 3: "Dock."

MOUSE: I'm ready.

PERSON 1: Hickory,

PERSON 2: Dickory,

PERSON 3: Dock.

PERSON 1: The Mouse

MOUSE: That's me!

PERSON 2: Ran up the clock.

PERSON 3: The clock struck one,

POSSIBLE CONCLUSIONS

1. The Mouse was scared of heights and began to scream and shout.

2. The Mouse didn't know how to tell time and missed recess.

3. When the Mouse got to the top he saw the Three Little Pigs and they decided to have a picnic.

4. The Mouse got very sick and had to go to the nurse's office.

5. Your idea.

Do Your Ears Hang Low?

STAGING: The characters should all be standing. The scripts should be placed on music stands (thus leaving the character's hands free to perform the motions indicated in the script). As each character finishes saying her or his line, the other characters perform the motion described in the script. There is no narrator for this script.

Abby	Bobbie	Cathy	David	Erin
X	X	X	X	X

ABBY: Do your ears hang low? [hands on side of head with fingers pointing down]

BOBBIE: Do they wobble to and fro? [wiggle fingers]

CATHY: Can you tie them in a knot? [simulate tying a large knot with hands]

DAVID: Can you tie them in a bow? [simulate tying a large bow with hands]

ERIN: Can you throw them o'er your shoulder like a Continental Soldier? [simulate throwing a large load over the right shoulder]

ALL: Do your ears hang low?

ABBY: Does your tongue hang down? [stick tongue out]

From *MORE Tadpole Tales and Other Totally Terrific Treats for Readers Theatre* by Anthony D. Fredericks. Santa Barbara, CA: Libraries Unlimited. Copyright © 2010.

BOBBIE: Does it flop all around? [wiggle tongue]

CATHY: Can you tie it in a knot? [simulate tying a large knot with hands]

DAVID: Can you tie it in a bow? [simulate tying a large bow with hands]

ERIN: Can you throw it o'er your shoulder like a Continental Soldier? [simulate throwing a large load over the right shoulder]

ALL: Does your tongue hang down?

POSSIBLE CONCLUSIONS

1. Use a variety of other body parts, including (but not limited to) nose, eyes, knees.

2. Focus on the various body parts of a popular figure (e.g., singer, actress, pop icon).

3. Use items found throughout the classroom (e.g., white board, pencils, desks).

4. Incorporate physical features of the school librarian, gym teacher, or principal.

5. Your idea.

Snow White and Her "Attitude"

STAGING: The narrator should be seated on a tall stool to the side of all the characters. The characters may be standing and moving around throughout the presentation.

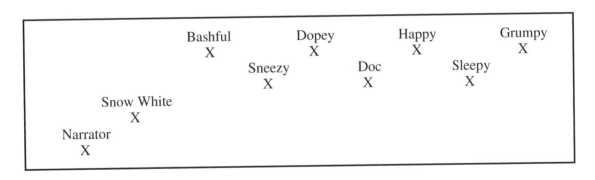

	Bashful X		Dopey X		Happy X		Grumpy X
		Sneezy X		Doc X		Sleepy X	
Snow White X							
Narrator X							

NARRATOR: Once upon a time, there were . . .

SNOW WHITE: [angry] Now, just wait a minute, buster. Let's get one thing straight. I'm the star of this production, right?

NARRATOR: Yeah, I guess so.

SNOW WHITE: [in a tough voice] Hey, you know so. Just so we get things right—let's be very clear. I'M THE STAR! And because I'm the star, I get top billing. Right?

From *MORE Tadpole Tales and Other Totally Terrific Treats for Readers Theatre* by Anthony D. Fredericks. Santa Barbara, CA: Libraries Unlimited. Copyright © 2010.

NARRATOR: OK, that's fine with me. But you see, as the official narrator for this story, I must set things up for the audience out there. [points to audience]

SNOW WHITE: [angry] That's fine with me, buster. But just don't take up a lot of my valuable time. I've got lots of important things to do. In other words, you better make it quick and you better make it short.

NARRATOR: OK, OK, just don't get your nose bent out of shape. Just give me a chance and I'll get this story moving along.

SNOW WHITE: You're on. But just so you know—I'm watching you! If I don't like where this story is going then, believe me, I'm outta here.

NARRATOR: I hear you, I hear you. So what do you say we get going on this little story of ours?

SNOW WHITE: OK, but it had better be good.

NARRATOR: OK, now where were we? Oh, now I remember. You see these guys over here [points to the seven dwarfs], we're going to start the story with them—you know, the part where they're working in the mine and where they are. . . .

SNOW WHITE: [angry] Now, just a gosh darn minute here. Didn't I tell you I was the star of this story? What are you doing starting this tale with these seven strange-looking characters over here? [points to dwarfs]

POSSIBLE CONCLUSIONS

1. Each of the seven dwarfs tells Snow White to "take a hike." They really don't need her "attitude" in the story.

2. Each of the seven dwarfs tells Snow White that she's really in the wrong story. She should be over helping Little Red Riding Hood deal with the Big Bad Wolf.

3. The narrator gets really upset with Snow White and her "attitude" and decides to leave the story.

4. A witch comes along and makes Snow White eat a poisoned apple. She sleeps for a thousand years and the seven dwarfs live happily ever after.

5. Your idea.

Jack and the Very Tall Bean Plant

STAGING: The narrator sits on a stool in front of the characters. The characters may be seated in chairs or standing. (The Giant will enter the story later.)

Jack	Mother		Giant	Cow
X	X		X	X
		Narrator		
		X		

NARRATOR: This is a story about Jack and a bean plant. You see, once upon a time Jack was a student in our class. But he did something that wasn't very bright and wasn't very smart. This story is his story.

JACK: [excited] Hey, Mom, guess what I did? I sold our cow at the grocery store. A very nice man gave me some bean seeds for good old Bessie, and now I think we're rich!.

NARRATOR: [to the audience] You should know that Jack isn't the brightest kid in school. Of course, everybody knows that you can't sell a cow at the grocery store.

From *MORE Tadpole Tales and Other Totally Terrific Treats for Readers Theatre* by Anthony D. Fredericks. Santa Barbara, CA: Libraries Unlimited. Copyright © 2010.

I mean, that would be stupid! And someone isn't going to give you some bean seeds for a cow. But this is a pretend story, so maybe we should just listen.

MOTHER: Jack, you are a silly, silly boy! What were you thinking? You sold our cow down at the grocery store. Didn't you hear what the narrator said? You can't sell cows at a grocery store.

JACK: Yeah, but this is a pretend story, so maybe it was a pretend cow and maybe these are some pretend bean seeds. Maybe we should just pretend that I did all that stuff.

COW: [to audience] Think how I feel. I give Jack and his mother lots of milk, and he goes and sells me at a pretend grocery store and then some pretend man gives him some pretend bean seeds. Man, I'm feeling really bad. Maybe we should just pretend that this story never happened and I can go back and just eat grass all day long.

NARRATOR: Then we wouldn't have a story to share. We would have to pretend there was a story and we would have to pretend there was a pretend cow and a pretend mother and a pretend Jack. So why don't we pretend not to pretend; then we could have a real story. . . not a pretend one!

MOTHER: Sounds good to me.

JACK: Me, too.

COW: Me, too.

MOTHER: OK, where were we? Oh, I remember—my silly, silly son just sold the cow at the grocery store and got some silly, silly bean seeds.

JACK: Yeah, now we don't have the cow, but we do have these silly, silly seeds. So what should we do now?

POSSIBLE CONCLUSIONS

1. Jack's mother throws the bean seeds out the window, and the next morning there is a giant bean plant outside. Jack and his mother cook up a big pot of baked beans.

2. Jack's mother throws the bean seeds out the window, and the next morning there is a giant bean plant outside. A big giant climbs down the bean plant and decides to stay for dinner.

3. Jack throws the bean seeds out the window, and a giant cow springs up from each seed.

4. Jack eats the bean seeds and turns into 1) a cow, 2) a giant, or 3) a teacher.

5. Your idea.

Chicken Little Gets Really Crazy

STAGING: The narrator may sit on a tall stool off to the side of the staging area. The other characters may sit on chairs or stools.

		Student 1 X	Student 2 X
	Chicken Little X		
		Student 3 X	Student 4 X
Narrator X			

CHICKEN LITTLE: [very excited] The math homework is coming! The math homework is coming!!

NARRATOR: Now, wait just a gosh darn minute here.

CHICKEN LITTLE: [extremely excited] The math homework is coming! The math homework is coming!!

NARRATOR: [impatient] Now, just hold on, will ya? I'm trying to set up this story. All you're doing is running around like some birdbrain. Just pipe down.

CHICKEN LITTLE: [really agitated] The math homework is coming! The math homework is coming!!

NARRATOR: Now, wait just a gosh darn minute here. I'm supposed to be the narrator in this story. That means I'm supposed to know all there is to know about this story. The way I remember it, Mr. Little here [points to Chicken Little] should be running around saying, "The sky is falling, the sky is falling."

CHICKEN LITTLE: [nervous] The math homework is coming! The math homework is coming!!

STUDENT 1: I think what he's saying is, "The math homework is coming!'

NARRATOR: I know what he's saying, silly. But why does he keep saying it over and over?

STUDENT 2: Maybe he's scared.

STUDENT 3: I think he's just afraid of all the work we get. I mean, it really is a lot of math homework.

STUDENT 4: Yeah, sometimes it just takes forever. Problem after problem after problem after. . . .

CHICKEN LITTLE: [nervous] The math homework is coming! The math homework is coming!!

STUDENT 1: Yeah, I don't know why our teacher gives us so much math homework. It just seems like it never stops. It just seems like it takes forever!

STUDENT 2: Why do teachers do that? Do they really think we'll get smarter if we do lots of math homework?

STUDENT 3: Why so much math homework every night? I barely have enough time to breathe.

CHICKEN LITTLE: [really agitated] The math homework is coming! The math homework is coming!!

STUDENT 4: You'd think that math homework was the most important thing in the world. Math, math, math—why do teachers have to give so much of it? Sometimes, it just never stops.

STUDENT 1: You're right. But you know, I think we have another problem here.

STUDENT 4: What's that?

POSSIBLE CONCLUSIONS

1. Chicken Little goes really crazy and starts yelling about the science homework and the social studies homework and the language arts homework and the . . . .

2. The teacher turns into the Big Bad Wolf and starts to huff and puff around the classroom.

3. Chicken Little starts a food fight in the cafeteria and begins to toss eggs all over the place.

4. Chicken Little falls over from sheer exhaustion and has to be carried down to the nurse's office.

5. Your idea.

APPENDIXES

**When You See This Section in a Book
You Know That the Book Is Almost Over
(Which Is Why This Part Is Always Placed
Near the End of the Book)**

Appendix A

Here's a Bunch of Fairy Tales, Mother Goose Rhymes, Folktales, and Other Really Neat Stories (from "Once Upon a Time" Time) to Share with Kids and Other Human Beings

Aesop. *Aesop's Fables.* New York: Viking, 1981.

Alderson, Brian, ed. *Cakes and Custard: Children's Rhymes.* New York: Morrow, 1975.

Anderson, Hans Christian. *Thumbelina.* New York: Dial, 1979.

———. *The Ugly Duckling.* New York: Harcourt Brace Jovanovich, 1979.

Asbjørnsen, Peter Christian, an E. Moe Jorgen. *Three Billy Goats Gruff.* New York: Clarion, 1981.

Brett, Jan. *Beauty and the Beast.* New York: Clarion, 1989.

———. *Goldilocks and the Three Bears.* New York: Dodd, Mead, 1987.

Briggs, Raymond. *The Mother Goose Treasury.* New York: Coward-McCann, 1966.

Brooke, William. *A Telling of the Tales.* New York: Harper & Row, 1990.

Cauley, Lorinda Bryan. *Goldilocks and the Three Bears.* New York: Putnam, 1981.

———. *The Town Mouse and the Country Mouse.* New York: Putnam, 1984.

Cohn, Amy. *From Sea to Shining Sea: A Treasury of American Folklore and Folk Songs.* New York: Scholastic, 1993.

Cole, Joanna, and Stephanie Calmenson. *Miss Mary Mac: And Other Children's Street Rhymes.* New York: Morrow, 1990.

Craig, Helen. *The Town Mouse and the Country Mouse.* Watertown, MA: Candlewick, 1992.

De Beaumont, Madame Le Prince. *Beauty and the Beast.* New York: Crown, 1986.

dePaola, Tomie. *The Comic Adventures of Old Mother Hubbard and Her Dog.* San Diego: Harcourt Brace Jovanovich, 1981.

———. *Tomie dePaola's Favorite Nursery Tales.* New York: Putnam, 1986.

———. *Tomie dePaola's Mother Goose.* New York: Putnam's, 1985.

De Regniers, Beatrice Schenk. *Red Riding Hood: Retold in Verse.* New York: Atheneum, 1977.

Domanska, Janina. *Little Red Hen.* New York: Macmillan, 1973.

Edens, Cooper, ed. *The Glorious Mother Goose.* New York: Atheneum, 1988.

Ehrlich, Amy. *Random House Book of Fairy Tales.* New York: Random, 1985.

Emberley, Barbara. *The Story of Paul Bunyan.* Englewood Cliffs, NJ: Prentice-Hall, 1963.

Evslin, Bernard. *Hercules.* New York: Morrow, 1984.

Fisher, Leonard Everett. *The Olympians: Great Gods and Goddesses of Ancient Greece.* New York: Holiday, 1984.

French, Fiona. *Snow White in New York.* New York: Oxford, 1987.

Galdone, Paul. *Cinderella.* New York: McGraw-Hill, 1978.

———. *The Gingerbread Boy.* New York: Clarion, 1983.

———. *The Hare and the Tortoise.* New York: McGraw-Hill, 1962.

———. *Henny Penny.* New York: Clarion, 1984.

———. *Jack and the Beanstalk.* New York: Clarion, 1982.

———. *Little Bo-Peep.* New York: Clarion, 1982.

———. *The Little Red Hen.* New York: McGraw-Hill, 1985.

———. *Little Red Riding Hood.* New York: McGraw-Hill, 1974.

———. *The Magic Porridge Pot.* New York: Clarion, 1976.

———. *Old Mother Hubbard and Her Dog.* New York: McGraw-Hill, 1960.

———. *Rumpelstiltskin.* New York: Clarion, 1985.

———. *Three Aesop Fox Fables.* New York: Clarion, 1971.

———. *The Three Bears.* New York: Clarion, 1985.

———. *Three Little Kittens.* New York: Clarion, 1986.

———. *The Three Little Pigs.* New York: Clarion, 1984.

Goode, Diane. *Diane Goode's Book of Silly Stories and Songs.* New York: Dutton, 1992.

Greenaway, Kate. *Mother Goose: Or, the Old Nursery Rhymes.* New York: Warne, 1981.

Griego, Margot C., Betsy L. Bucks, Sharon S. Gilbert, and Laurel H. Kimball. *Tortillas Para Mama and Other Spanish Nursery Rhymes.* New York: Holt, Rinehart & Winston, 1981.

Grimm, Jakob, and Wilhelm Grimm. *The Bremen Town Musicians.* New York: Harper & Row, 1987.

———. *Cinderella.* New York: Greenwillow, 1981.

———. *The Donkey Prince.* New York: Doubleday, 1977.

———. *The Elves and the Shoemaker.* Chicago: Follett, 1967.

———. *Favorite Tales from Grimm.* New York: Four Winds, 1982.

———. *The Frog Prince.* New York: Scholastic, 1987.

———. *Grimm's Fairy Tales: Twenty Stories Illustrated by Arthur Rackham.* New York: Viking, 1973.

———. *Hansel and Gretel.* New York: Morrow, 1980.

———. *Little Red Riding Hood.* New York: Atheneum, 1988.

———. *Popular Folk Tales: The Brothers Grimm.* New York: Doubleday, 1978.

———. *Rapunzel.* New York: Holiday House, 1987.

———. *Rumpelstiltskin.* New York: Four Winds, 1973.

———. *The Shoemaker and the Elves.* New York: Lothrop, 1983.

———. *The Sleeping Beauty.* New York: Atheneum, 1979.

———. *Snow White.* Boston: Little, Brown, 1974.

———. *Snow White and Rose Red.* New York: Delacorte, 1965.

———. *Snow White and the Seven Dwarfs.* New York: Farrar, 1987.

———. *Tom Thumb.* New York: Walck, 1974.

Hague, Michael, ed. *Mother Goose.* New York: Holt, Rinehart & Winston, 1984.

Hale, Sara. *Mary Had a Little Lamb.* New York: Holiday House, 1984.

Haley, Gail. *Jack and the Bean Tree.* New York: Crown, 1986.

Harper, Wilhelmina. *The Gunniwolf.* New York: Dutton, 1967.

Hastings, Selina. *Sir Gawain and the Loathly Lady.* New York: Lothrop, Lee & Shepard, 1985.

Hayes, Sarah. *Bad Egg: The True Story of Humpty Dumpty.* Boston: Little, Brown, 1987.

Hodges, Margaret. *Saint George and the Dragon.* Boston: Little, Brown, 1984.

Huck, Charlotte. *Princess Furball.* New York: Greenwillow, 1989.

Hutchinson, Veronica S. *Henny Penny.* Boston: Little, Brown, 1976.

Hutton, Warwick. *Beauty and the Beast.* New York: Atheneum, 1985.

Ivimey, John W. *The Complete Story of the Three Blind Mice.* New York: Clarion, 1987.

Jacobs, Joseph. *Jack and the Beanstalk.* New York: Putnam's, 1983.

———. *The Three Little Pigs.* New York: Atheneum, 1980.

Jeffers, Susan. *If Wishes Were Horses: Mother Goose Rhymes.* New York: Dutton, 1979.

Kellogg, Steven. *Chicken Little.* New York: Morrow, 1985.

———. *Paul Bunyan.* New York: Morrow, 1974.

———. *Johnny Appleseed.* New York: Morrow, 1988.

———. *Pecos Bill.* New York: Morrow, 1986.

———. *Mike Fink.* New York: Morrow, 1992.

Kimmel, Eric. *The Gingerbread Man.* New York: Holiday, 1993.

Kingsley, Charles. *The Heroes.* New York: Mayflower, 1980.

Lobel, Arnold. *Gregory Griggs and Other Nursery Rhyme People.* New York: Greenwillow, 1978

———. *The Random House Book of Mother Goose.* New York: Random House, 1986.

Marshall, James. *Goldilocks and the Three Bears.* New York: Dial, 1988.

———. *Hansel and Gretel.* New York: Dial, 1990.

———. *James Marshall's Mother Goose.* New York: Farrar, Straus & Giroux, 1979.

———. *Red Riding Hood.* New York: Dial, 1987.

Martin, Sarah. *The Comic Adventures of Old Mother Hubbard and Her Dog.* San Diego: Harcourt Brace, 1981.

McKinley, Robin. *The Outlaws of Sherwood.* New York: Greenwillow, 1988.

Miles, Bernard. *Robin Hood: His Life and Legend.* New York: Hamlyn, 1979.

Miller, Mitchell. *One Misty Moisty Morning.* New York: Farrar, Straus & Giroux, 1971.

Newbery, John. *The Original Mother Goose's Melody.* New York: Gale, 1969.

Opie, Iona, and Peter Opie. *A Nursery Companion.* London: Oxford University Press, 1980.

———. *The Oxford Nursery Rhyme Book.* London, Oxford University Press, 1984.

———. *Tail Feathers from Mother Goose: The Opie Rhyme Book.* Boston: Little, Brown, 1988.

Ormerod, Jan. *The Story of Chicken Licken.* New York: Lothrop, 1986.

Oxenbury, Helen. *The Helen Oxenbury Nursery Story Book.* New York: Knopf, 1985.

Pearson, Tracey. *Old Macdonald Had a Farm.* New York: Dial, 1984.

Perrault, Charles. *Cinderella.* New York: Dial, 1985.

———. *Little Red Riding Hood.* New York: Scholastic, 1971.

———. *Puss in Boots.* New York: Clarion, 1976.

———. *The Sleeping Beauty.* New York: Viking, 1972.

Provensen, Alice, and Martin Provensen. *Old Mother Hubbard.* New York: Random House, 1982.

Riordan, James. *Tales of King Arthur.* New York: Rand McNally, 1982.

Rounds, Glen. *Old Macdonald Has a Farm.* New York: Holiday House, 1989.

———. *Three Little Pigs and the Big Bad Wolf.* New York: Holiday, 1992.

Scieszka, Jon. *The Stinky Cheese Man and Other Fairly Stupid Tales.* New York: Viking, 1992.

———. *The True Story of the 3 Little Pigs.* New York: Viking, 1989.

Southey, Robert. *The Three Bears.* New York: Putnam's, 1984.

Spier, Peter. *London Bridge Is Falling Down.* New York: Doubleday, 1967.

Stevens, Janet. *Goldilocks and the Three Bears.* New York: Holiday House, 1986.

———. *The House That Jack Built.* New York: Holiday House, 1985.

———. *The Tortoise and the Hare.* New York: Holiday House, 1984.

———. *The Town Mouse and the Country Mouse.* New York: Holiday House, 1987.

Still, James. *Jack and the Wonder Beans.* New York: Putnam's, 1977.

Stoutenburg, Adrien. *American Tall Tales.* New York: Viking, 1966.

Tarrant, Margaret. *Nursery Rhymes.* New York: Crowell, 1978.

Thompson, Pat, ed. *Rhymes Around the Day.* New York: Lothrop, Lee & Shepard, 1983.

Tripp, Wallace. *Granfa' Grig Had a Pig and Other Rhymes Without Reason from Mother Goose.* Boston: Little, Brown, 1976.

Tudor, Tasha. *Mother Goose.* New York: Walck, 1972.

Watson, Wendy. *Wendy Watson's Mother Goose.* New York: Lothrop, Lee & Shepard, 1989.

Watts, Bernadette. *Goldilocks and the Three Bears.* New York: Holt, Rinehart & Winston, 1985.

Wildsmith, Brian. *Brian Wildsmith's Mother Goose.* New York: Oxford University Press, 1982.

Willard, Nancy. *Beauty and the Beast.* New York: Harcourt Brace Jovanovich, 1992.

Zemach, Harve. *Duffy and the Devil.* New York: Farrar, Straus & Giroux, 1973.

Zuromskis, Diane. *The Farmer in the Dell.* Boston: Little, Brown, 1978.

Appendix B

WOW! This Is Unbelievable! Here's a List of Several Far-Out and Funky Titles Students Can Use to Create Their Own Readers Theatre Scripts (from Scratch, No Less)

1. Our Teacher Is the Most Beautiful and Most Intelligent Person in the Entire World (and/or Universe)

2. Our Librarian Is the Most Beautiful and Most Intelligent Person in the Entire World (and/or Universe)

3. Our Teacher Marries a Rich and Handsome Prince (or Beautiful Princess)

4. Our Librarian Marries a Rich and Handsome Prince (or BeautifulPrincess)

5. Our Teacher Never Never, Ever Ever Gives Math Homework Again!

6. Mother Goose Is Really a Duck (or Perhaps a Really Strange Bird)

7. "Don't You Dare Touch My Foot," Cinderella Yells to the Handsome Prince

8. Mary Had a Little Octopus (She Couldn't Find Her Lamb)

9. Sleeping Beauty Never Wakes Up (She Just Keeps Snoring for about a Thousand Years or So)

10. The Three Billy Goats Gruff Get an Attitude Adjustment

11. Thumbelina and Tom Thumb Are Not Really Twins, They Just Have Funny-Sounding Names

12. Red Riding Hood, Green Jumping Cape, and Blue Trotting Coat Teach the Wolf a Lesson He'll Never Forget

13. Hansel and Gretel Change Their Names and Become Finalists on *American Idol*®.

14. The Three Bears Move Out of the Cottage and into a Condo in the City

15. Little Miss Muffet Goes Crazy and Starts Beating Up all the Insects in the Forest

16. The Enchanted Prince Gets Kissed by the Evil Witch and Changes His Life Forever

17. Paul Bunyan Stubs His Toe and Starts to Cry

18. Chicken Little Gets Fried for Dinner

19. The Prince Finds Cinderella's Glass Slipper and Boy, Does It Stink!

20. Mary Had a Little Lamb, a Little Turkey, a Little Chicken, and a Little Roast Beef—and She Was Still Hungry!

21. The Tortoise and the Hare Fall in Love (Hint: It's Not Pretty!)

22. Goldilocks Goes on Trial for Breaking and Entering

23. Sleeping Beauty and the Giant Hippopotamus

24. A Stack of Pancakes, Two Sausage Links, Orange Juice, Buttered Toast, and Humpty Dumpty on the Side

25. Baa Baa Black Sheep, Neigh Neigh Orange Horse, Woof Woof Purple Dog, Meow Meow Crimson Cat

26. The Three Blind Mice Go to the Optometrist and Get Some Really Cool Glasses

27. Why the Heck Do We Keep Going Round and Round the Stupid Mulberry Bush?

28. Little Miss Muffet Eats a Whole Lot of Snickers Bars 'Cause She Just Doesn't Like Curds and Whey Anymore

29. This Little Piggy Said, "I'm Really Tired of Going Wee-Wee-Wee All Day Long!"

30. Little Jack Horner Sat in a Corner Eating Some Cheese Whiz®

31. Jack Climbs to the Top of the Beanstalk and Sees Something Really Disgusting

32. Snow White Redecorates Peter Pumpkin-eater's House

33. The Three Billy Goats Gruff Start Dating the Three Little Pigs

34. One, Two, Buckle My Shoe; Three, Four, Our Teacher Can Snore!

35. One, Two, Buckle My Shoe; Three, Four, Our Librarian Can Snore!

36. One, Two, Buckle My Shoe; Three, Four, Our Principal Can Snore!

37. Cinderella—World Wide Wrestling Champion!

38. Little Boy Blue Marries Little Red Riding Hood and Little Purple Baby Is Born

39. Old King Cole Decided He Wasn't Merry Anymore

40. Rumpelstiltskin Changes His Name to Bill (or Sam or Tom or Ken)

41. Roses Are Red, Violets Are Blue, Our Teacher is Very, Very Crazy, and So Are You

42. Mary Had a Little Lamb Who Grew up to Become a Very Bad Sheep with an Attitude Problem

43. Georgie Porgie, Pudding and Pie, Kissed the Girls and Got into a Lot of Trouble with the Principal

44. Beauty and the Beast Get Married and Honeymoon in Hawaii

45. The Ugly Duckling Enters a Beauty Pageant

46. Rapunzel Loses Her Hair

47. Paul Bunyan Gets Really Hungry and Eats Denver

48. Dragons are Just Alligators with Cool Costumes

49. Alice in Wonderland Teaches Second Grade

50. The Emperor Gets All His New Clothes at Wal-Mart

51. The Frog Prince Starts Pumping Iron (Watch Out!)

52. The Evil Stepmother Finally Figures Out Why Nobody Likes Her

53. The Goose That Laid the Golden Egg Is Really a Porcupine in Disguise

54. Jack Grows Some Sweet Peas, Carrots, and Broccoli Instead of a Beanstalk

55. Peter Pan Gets Arrested for Flying Over the White House

56. Pinocchio Gets a Nose Job

57. The Seven Dwarfs Star in a New Pirate Movie.

58. "Kiss My Slime, Tadpole!"

59. A "Once Upon a Time" Story That Really Happened

60. If You Think the Fire-Breathing Dragon Is Bad, Wait Till You See Our Teacher

61. How to Barbeque the Three Little Pigs—Hints for the Busy Cook

62. Jack and Jill Hurt Themselves Really Bad

63. Our Principal—A True Prince Charming

64. Donald Gets in Touch with His Inner Duck

65. Watch Out! The Wolves Are in Town.

66. The Cafeteria Lady Is Really a Wicked Witch Who Eats Children

67. "Short Men Are Real Slobs," Snow White Mutters One Day

68. The Three Bears Learn How to Read

Appendix C

Here Are Some Other Really Amazing and Absolutely Incredible Readers Theatre Resources You Might Want to Look at (in Addition to the Really Amazing and Absolutely Incredible *MORE Tadpole Tales and Other Totally Terrific Treats for Readers Theatre*)

READERS THEATRE BOOKS

Barchers, S. *Fifty Fabulous Fables: Beginning Readers Theatre*. Santa Barbara, CA: Teacher Ideas Press, 1997.

———. *From Atalanta to Zeus*. Santa Barbara, CA: Teacher Ideas Press, 2001.

———. *Judge for Yourself*. Santa Barbara, CA: Teacher Ideas Press, 2004.

———. *Multicultural Folktales: Readers Theatre for Elementary Students*. Santa Barbara, CA: Teacher Ideas Press, 2000.

———. *Readers Theatre for Beginning Readers*. Santa Barbara, CA: Teacher Ideas Press, 1993.

———. *Scary Readers Theatre*. Santa Barbara, CA: Teachers Ideas Press, 1994.

Barchers, S., and J. L. Kroll. *Classic Readers Theatre for Young Adults*. Santa Barbara, CA: Teacher Ideas Press, 2002.

Barchers, S., and C. R. Pfeffinger. *More Readers Theatre for Beginning Readers*. Santa Barbara, CA: Teacher Ideas Press, 2006.

Barnes, J. W. *Sea Songs*. Santa Barbara, CA: Teacher Ideas Press, 2004.

Black, A. N. *Born Storytellers*. Santa Barbara, CA: Teacher Ideas Press, 2005.

Criscoe, B. L., and P. J. Lanasa. *Fairy Tales for Two Readers*. Santa Barbara, CA: Teacher Ideas Press, 1995.

Dixon, N., A. Davies, and C. Politano. *Learning with Readers Theatre: Building Connections*. Winnipeg, Canada: Peguis Publishers, 1996.

Fredericks, Anthony D. *African Legends, Myths, and Folktales for Readers Theatre*. Santa Barbara, CA: Teacher Ideas Press, 2008.

———. *Building Fluency with Readers Theatre: Motivational Strategies, Successful Lessons and Dynamic Scripts to Develop Fluency, Comprehension, Writing, and Vocabulary*. Santa Barbara, CA: Teacher Ideas Press, 2008.

———. *Fairy Tales Readers Theatre*. Santa Barbara, CA: Teacher Ideas Press, 2009.

———. *Frantic Frogs and Other Frankly Fractured Folktales for Readers Theatre*. Santa Barbara, CA: Teacher Ideas Press, 1993.

———. *MORE Frantic Frogs and Other Frankly Fractured Folktales for Readers Theatre*. Santa Barbara, CA: Teacher Ideas Press, 2008.

———. *Mother Goose Readers Theatre for Beginning Readers*. Santa Barbara, CA: Teacher Ideas Press, 2007.

———. *Nonfiction Readers Theatre for Beginning Readers*. Santa Barbara, CA: Teacher Ideas Press, 2007.

———. *Readers Theatre for American History*. Santa Barbara, CA: Teacher Ideas Press, 2001.

———. *Science Fiction Readers Theatre*. Santa Barbara, CA: Teacher Ideas Press, 2002.

———. *Silly Salamanders and Other Slightly Stupid Stories for Readers Theatre*. Santa Barbara, CA: Teacher Ideas Press, 2000.

———. *Songs and Rhymes Readers Theatre for Beginning Readers*. Santa Barbara, CA: Teacher Ideas Press, 2007.

———. *Tadpole Tales and Other Totally Terrific Treats for Readers Theatre*. Santa Barbara, CA: Teacher Ideas Press, 1997.

Garner, J. *Wings of Fancy: Using Readers Theatre to Study Fantasy Genre*. Santa Barbara, CA: Teacher Ideas Press, 2006

Georges, C., and C. Cornett. *Reader's Theatre*. Buffalo, NY: D.O.K. Publishers, 1990.

Haven, K. *Great Moments in Science: Experiments and Readers Theatre*. Santa Barbara, CA: Teacher Ideas Press, 1996.

Jenkins, D. R. *Just Deal with It*. Santa Barbara, CA: Teacher Ideas Press, 2004.

Johnson, T. D., and D. R. Louis. *Bringing It All Together: A Program for Literacy*. Portsmouth, NH: Heinemann, 1990.

Kroll, J. L. *Simply Shakespeare*. Santa Barbara, CA: Teacher Ideas Press, 2003.

Latrobe, K. H., C. Casey, and L. A. Gann. *Social Studies Readers Theatre for Young Adults*. Santa Barbara, CA: Teacher Ideas Press, 1991.

Laughlin, M. K., P. T. Black, and K. H. Latrobe. *Social Studies Readers Theatre for Children*. Santa Barbara, CA: Teacher Ideas Press, 1991.

Laughlin, M. K., and K. H. Latrobe. *Readers Theatre for Children*. Santa Barbara, CA: Teacher Ideas Press, 1990.

Martin, J. M. *12 Fabulously Funny Fairy Tale Plays*. New York: Instructor Books, 2002.

Peterson, C. *Around the World Through Holidays*. Santa Barbara, CA: Teacher Ideas Press, 2005.

Pfeffinger, C. R. *Character Counts*. Santa Barbara, CA: Teacher Ideas Press, 2003.

———. *Holiday Readers Theatre*. Santa Barbara, CA: Teacher Ideas Press, 1994.

Pugliano-Martin, C. *25 Just-Right Plays for Emergent Readers (Grades K–1)*. New York: Scholastic, 1999.

Shepard, A. *Folktales on Stage: Children's Plays for Readers Theatre.* Olympia, WA: Shepard Publications, 2003.

———. *Readers on Stage: Resources for Readers Theatre.* Olympia, WA: Shepard Publications, 2004.

———. *Stories on Stage: Children's Plays for Readers Theatre.* Olympia, WA: Shepard Publications, 2005.

Sloyer, S. *From the Page to the Stage.* Santa Barbara, CA: Teacher Ideas Press, 2003.

Smith, C. *Extraordinary Women from U.S. History.* Santa Barbara, CA: Teacher Ideas Press, 2003.

Wolf, J. M. *Cinderella Outgrows the Glass Slipper and Other Zany Fractured Fairy Tale Plays.* New York: Scholastic, 2002.

Wolfman, J. *How and Why Stories for Readers Theatre.* Santa Barbara, CA: Teacher Ideas Press, 2004.

Worthy, J. *Readers Theatre for Building Fluency: Strategies and Scripts for Making the Most of This Highly Effective, Motivating, and Research-Based Approach to Oral Reading.* New York: Scholastic, 2005.

WEB SITES

http://www.aaronshep.com/rt/RTE.html

How to use readers theatre, sample scripts from a children's author who specializes in readers theatre, and an extensive list of resources.

http://www.cdli.ca/CITE/langrt.htm

This site has lots of information, including What is Readers Theatre, Readers Theatre Scripts, Writing Scripts, Recommended Print Resources, and Recommended On-line Resources.

http://www.teachingheart.net/readerstheater.htm

Here you discover lots of plays and scripts to print and read in your classroom or library.

http://literacyconnections.com/readerstheater

There is an incredible number of resources and scripts at this all-inclusive site.

http://www.proteacher.com/070173.shmtl

This site is a growing collection of tens of thousands of ideas shared by teachers across the United States and around the world.

http://www.readerstheatredigest.com

This is an online magazine of ideas, scripts, and teaching strategies.

http://www.readerstheatre.escd.net

This site has over 150 small poems, stories, and chants for readers theatre.

http://www.storycart.com

Storycart's Press's subscription service provides an inexpensive opportunity to have timely scripts delivered to teachers or librarians each month. Each script is created or adapted by well-known writer Suzanne Barchers, author of several readers theatre books (see above).

PROFESSIONAL ORGANIZATIONS

Institute for Readers Theatre
P.O. Box 421262
San Diego, CA 92142
(858) 277-4274
http://www.readerstheatreinstitute.com

Appendix D

The Stuff the Author Person Consulted When He Was Doing His Research for This Book, Which Always Gets Put at the Very End of Any Book (But That Doesn't Mean This Stuff Isn't Important)

Cunningham, P., and R. Allington. 2003. *Classrooms That Work: They Can All Read and Write.* Boston: Allyn & Bacon.

Dixon, N., A. Davies, and C. Politano. 1996. *Learning with Readers Theatre: Building Connections.* Winnipeg, Canada: Peguis Publishers.

Fredericks, A. D. 1993. *Frantic Frogs and Other Frankly Fractured Folktales for Readers Theatre.* Santa Barbara, CA: Teacher Ideas Press.

———. 2001. *Guided Reading for Grades 3–6.* Austin, TX: Harcourt Achieve.

———. 2007. *Nonfiction Readers Theatre for Beginning Readers.* Santa Barbara, CA: Teacher Ideas Press.

———. 2008a. *MORE Frantic Frogs and Other Frankly Fractured Folktales for Readers Theatre.* Santa Barbara, CA: Teacher Ideas Press.

———. 2008b. *African Legends, Myths, and Folktales for Readers Theatre.* Santa Barbara, CA: Teacher Ideas Press.

Martinez, M., N. Roser, and S. Strecker. 1999. "I Never Thought I Could Be a Star": A Readers Theatre Ticket to Reading Fluency. *The Reading Teacher* 52: 326–34.

Meinbach, A. M., A. D. Fredericks, and L. Rothlein. 2000. *The Complete Guide to Thematic Units: Creating the Integrated Curriculum.* Norwood, MA: Christopher-Gordon Publishers.

Rasinski, T. V. 2003. *The Fluent Reader: Oral Reading Strategies for Building Word Recognition, Fluency, and Comprehension.* New York: Scholastic.

Strecker, S. K., N. L. Roser, and M. G. Martinez. 1999. "Toward Understanding Oral Reading Fluency." *Yearbook of the National Reading Conference* 48: 295–310.

Tyler, B., and D. J. Chard. 2000. "Using Readers Theatre to Foster Fluency in Struggling Readers: A Twist on the Repeated Reading Strategy." *Reading and Writing Quarterly* 16: 163–68.

Wiggens, G., and J. McTighe. 1998. *Understanding by Design.* Alexandria, VA: Association for Supervision and Curriculum Development.

Wiske, M. S., ed. 1998. *Teaching for Understanding.* San Francisco, CA: Jossey-Bass.

Wolf, S. 1998. "The Flight of Reading: Shifts in Instruction, Orchestration, and Attitudes Through Classroom Theatre." *Reading Research Quarterly* 33: 382–415.

Appendix E

A Whole Bunch of Other Books the Author Person Wrote That You May Be Interested in Having in Your Classroom or School Library, Which Will Definitely Make You the Coolest Teacher or Librarian in the State

The following books are all available from Teacher Ideas Press/ABC-CLIO (130 Cremona Drive, Santa Barbara, CA 93116); 1-800-368-6868; http://www.teacherideaspress.com).

African Legends, Myths, and Folktales for Readers Theatre. ISBN 978-1-59158-633-3. (166pp.; $25.00).

> Teachers are continually looking for materials that will enhance the study of cultures around the world. This collection of readers theatre scripts offers just that through an approach to the cultural study of Africa that will be fun and motivational for students and improve their reading fluency.

Building Fluency with Readers Theatre: Motivational Strategies, Successful Lessons and Dynamic Scripts to Develop Fluency, Comprehension, Writing, and Vocabulary. ISBN 978-1-59158-733-0. (225pp.; $35.00).

> Packed with practical ideas and loads of creative strategies, this resource offers teachers and librarians a wealth of innovative and dynamic techniques to stimulate and support the teaching of reading fluency across the elementary curriculum. This book is filled with the latest information, up-to-date data, and lots of inventive scripts for any classroom or library.

Fairy Tales Readers Theatre. ISBN 978-1-59158-849-8. (140pp.; $25.00).

> "Beauty and the Beast" . . . "Snow White" . . . "Goldilocks". Now you can bring the magic of some of the world's most timeless stories into your classroom or library. This book provides teachers and librarians with a dynamic compendium of 19 famous fairy tales, plus 6 slightly irreverent variations thereof, in a format guaranteed to excite, amuse, and delight every youngster.

Frantic Frogs and Other Frankly Fractured Folktales for Readers Theatre. ISBN 1-56308-174-1. (123pp.; $19.50).

> Have you heard "Don't Kiss Sleeping Beauty, She's Got Really Bad Breath" or "The Brussels Sprouts Man (The Gingerbread Man's Unbelievably Strange Cousin)"? This resource (grades 4–8) offers 30 reproducible satirical scripts for rip-roaring dramatics in any classroom or library.

The Integrated Curriculum: Books for Reluctant Readers, Grades 2–5. 2nd ed. ISBN 0-87287-994-1. (220pp.; $22.50).

This book presents guidelines for motivating and using literature with reluctant readers. The book contains more than 40 book units on titles carefully selected to motivate the most reluctant readers.

Investigating Natural Disasters Through Children's Literature: An Integrated Approach. ISBN 1-56308-861-4. (193pp.; $28.00).

Tap into students' inherent awe of storms, volcanic eruptions, hurricanes, earthquakes, tornadoes, floods, avalanches, landslides, and tsunamis to open their minds to the wonders and power of the natural world.

Involving Parents Through Children's Literature: P–K. ISBN 1-56308-022-2. (86pp.; $15.00).

Involving Parents Through Children's Literature: Grades 1–2. ISBN 1-56308-012-5. (95pp.; $14.50).

Involving Parents Through Children's Literature: Grades 3–4. ISBN 1-56308-013-3. (96pp.; $15.50).

Involving Parents Through Children's Literature: Grades 5–6. ISBN 1-56308-014-1. (107pp.; $16.00).

This series of four books offers engaging activities for adults and children that stimulate comprehension and promote reading enjoyment. Reproducible activity sheets based on high-quality children's books are designed in a convenient format so that children can take them home.

The Librarian's Complete Guide to Involving Parents Through Children's Literature: Grades K–6. ISBN 1-56308-538-0. (137pp.; $24.50).

Activities for 101 children's books are presented in a reproducible format, so librarians can distribute them to students to take home and share with parents.

MORE Frantic Frogs and Other Frankly Fractured Folktales for Readers Theatre. ISBN 978-1-59158-628-9. (154pp.; $25.00).

Remember all the fun you had with the original *Frantic Frogs*? Well, they're back!! Here's another laugh-fest overflowing with scripts that will leave students (and teachers) rolling in the aisles. (Don't miss "The Original Hip-Hop [by Busta Frog].")

MORE Science Adventures with Children's Literature: Reading Comprehension and Inquiry-Based Science. ISBN 978-1-59158-619-7. (443pp.; $35.00).

Get ready for hundreds of "hands-on, minds-on" projects that will actively engage students in positive learning experiences. Each of the 62 units offers book summaries, science topic areas, critical thinking questions, classroom resources, reproducible pages, and lots of easy-to-do activities, including science experiments for every grade level.

MORE Social Studies Through Children's Literature: An Integrated Approach. ISBN 1-56308-761-8. (225pp.; $27.50).

Energize your social studies curriculum with dynamic, "hands-on, minds-on" projects based on such great children's books as *Amazing Grace*, *Fly Away Home*, and *Lon Po Po*. This book is filled with an array of activities and projects sure to "energize" any social studies curriculum.

Mother Goose Readers Theatre for Beginning Readers. ISBN 978-1-59158-500-8. (168pp.; $25.00).

Designed especially for educators in the primary grades, this resource provides engaging opportunities that capitalize on children's enjoyment of Mother Goose rhymes. There's lots to share and lots to enjoy in the pages of this resource.

MUCH MORE Social Studies Through Children's Literature: A Collaborative Approach. ISBN 978-1-59158-445-2. (256pp.; $35.00).

This collection of dynamic, literature-based activities will help any teacher or librarian energize the entire social studies curriculum and implement national (and state) standards. This resource is filled with hundreds of "hands-on, minds-on" projects.

Nonfiction Readers Theatre for Beginning Readers. ISBN 978-1-59158-499-5. (220pp.; $25.00).

This collection of science and social studies nonfiction scripts for beginning readers is sure to "jazz up" any language arts program in grades 1–3. Teachers and librarians will discover a wealth of creative opportunities to enhance fluency, comprehension, and appreciation of nonfiction literature.

Readers Theatre for American History. ISBN 1-56308-860-6. (173pp.; $30.00).

This book offers a participatory approach to American history in which students become active participants in several historical events. These 24 scripts give students a "you are there" perspective on critical milestones and colorful moments that have shaped the American experience.

Science Adventures with Children's Literature: A Thematic Approach. ISBN 1-56308-417-1. (190pp.; $24.50).

Focusing on the National Science Education Standards, this activity-centered resource uses a wide variety of children's literature to integrate science across the elementary curriculum. With a thematic approach, it features the best in science trade books along with stimulating "hands-on, minds-on" activities in all the sciences.

Science Discoveries on the Net: An Integrated Approach. ISBN 1-56308-823-1. (315pp.; $27.50).

This book is designed to help teachers integrate the Internet into their science programs and enhance the scientific discoveries of students. The 88 units emphasize key concepts—based on national and state standards—throughout the science curriculum.

Silly Salamanders and Other Slightly Stupid Stuff for Readers Theatre. ISBN 1-56308-825-8. (161pp.; $23.50).

The third entry in the "wild and wacky" readers theatre trilogy is just as crazy and just as weird as the first two. This unbelievable resource offers students in grades 3–6 dozens of silly send-ups of well-known fairy tales, legends, and original stories.

Social Studies Discoveries on the Net: An Integrated Approach. ISBN 1-56308-824-X. (276pp.; $26.00).

> This book is designed to help teachers integrate the Internet into their social studies programs and enhance the classroom discoveries of students. The 75 units emphasize key concepts—based on national and state standards—throughout the social studies curriculum.

Social Studies Through Children's Literature: An Integrated Approach. ISBN 1-87287-970-4. (192pp.; $24.00).

> Each of the 32 instructional units contained in this resource utilizes an activity-centered approach to elementary social studies, featuring children's picture books such as *Ox-Cart Man, In Coal Country,* and *Jambo Means Hello.*

Songs and Rhymes Readers Theatre for Beginning Readers. ISBN 978-1-59158-627-2. (154pp.; $25.00).

> Bring music, song, and dance into your classroom language arts curriculum with this delightful collection of popular rhymes and ditties. Beginning readers will enjoy learning about familiar characters in this engaging collection of scripts.

Tadpole Tales and Other Totally Terrific Titles for Readers Theatre. ISBN 1-56308-547-X. (115pp.; $18.50).

> A follow-up volume to the best-selling *Frantic Frogs and Other Frankly Fractured Folktales for Readers Theatre*, this book provides primary level readers (grades 1–4) with a humorous assortment of wacky tales based on well-known Mother Goose rhymes. More than 30 scripts and dozens of extensions will keep students rolling in the aisles.

Hey, that's a lot of books! Don't you think the author person should, like, get a life?

Index

About the Author Person

Anthony D. Fredericks
afredericks60@comcast.net

There will undoubtedly be many sharp-eyed readers who are now saying, "You know, I can see why he loves tadpoles so much—he looks sorta . . . well, he looks sorta . . . amphibious!" Of course, through the clever use of a certain software package we've been able to put a human face on him, plop some glasses on his nose, give him a full head of hair, and take at least two decades off his age (in tadpole years, he's actually 238 years old). Nevertheless, it should be quite obvious that this author guy is no enchanted prince. He does, however, have that incessant smile plastered on his face—but so do a lot of insurance salesmen and used car dealers.

Here's some stuff we do know about Tony: His background includes over 40 years of experience as a classroom teacher, reading specialist, curriculum coordinator, staff developer, professional storyteller, and college professor. (Yeah, he must be really, really old!) He is a prolific author, having written more than 75 teacher resource books, including the enormously popular *Nonfiction Readers Theatre for Beginning Readers,* the best-selling *Mother Goose Readers Theatre for Beginning Readers,* the celebrated *MUCH MORE Social Studies Through Children's Literature*, and the dynamic *MORE Science Adventures with Children's Literature.*

In addition, he has authored more than three dozen award-winning children's books, including *The Tsunami Quilt: Grandfather's Story*; *Near One Cattail: Turtles, Logs and Leaping Frogs*; *P Is for Prairie Dog: A Prairie Alphabet*; *Under One Rock: Bugs, Slugs and Other Ughs*; and *A Is for Anaconda: A Rainforest Alphabet.*

He's also written several best-selling (and very funny) adult nonfiction books, including *How Long Things Live* and *Walking with Dinosaurs.*

Tony currently teaches elementary methods courses in reading, language arts, science, social studies, and children's literature at York College in York, Pennsylvania (where his undergraduate students have other names for him besides "amphibian" or "Mr. Tadpole"). He is also a popular and enthusiastic visiting children's author at elementary schools throughout North America, where he celebrates writing with a whole new generation of young authors. During his school visits he is well-prepared to answer the four most-asked questions of every children's author: (1) "Where do you get your ideas?" (2) "How much money do you make?" (3) "How old are you?" and (4) "Is your wife pretty?"